I0540801

AWAKEN, ISRAEL

"The sun will be turned into darkness
And the moon into blood
Before the great
and awesome day of the LORD comes.
And it will come about that
whoever calls on the name of the LORD
Will be delivered;
For on Mount Zion and in Jerusalem
There will be those who escape,
As the LORD has said,
Even among the survivors
whom the LORD calls"
(Joel 2:31-32).

AWAKEN, ISRAEL

Dr. Jaerock Lee

URIM
BOOKS

AWAKEN, ISRAEL by Dr. Jaerock Lee

Published by Urim Books (Representative: Kyungtae Noh)
73, Yeouidaebang-ro 22-gil, Dongjak-Gu, Seoul, Korea
www.urimbooks.com

Previously published in Korean by Urim Books, Seoul, Korea.
Copyright © 2007, ISBN: 978-89-7557-141-1 (03230)
ISBN(CD-ROM): 978-89-7557-126-8 (08230)
Translated by Dr. Kooyoung Chung. Used by permission.

First Published February 2008

Edited by Dr. Geumsun Vin
Published in Seoul Korea by Urim Books
Printed in Seoul, Korea

TABLE OF CONTENTS

Preface

Foreword

Compliment

PREFACE

At the dawn of the 20th century, a remarkable series of events took place in the barren land of Palestine in which no one desired to live at the time. The Jews who had been scattered throughout Eastern Europe, Russia, and the rest of the globe began flocking to a land abounding in thistles, poverty, starvation, disease, and torment.

Despite a high rate of fatality resulting from malaria and starvation, the Jews did not fail to lose their high degree of faith and ambitions but commenced to build kibbutz (a place of work in Israel, for example a farm or factory, where the workers live together and share all the duties and income). Just as Theodor Herzl, the founder of modern Zionism, argued, "If you will it, it is no dream," the restoration of Israel became a reality.

In all fairness, the restoration of Israel was deemed an impossible dream to be achieved and no one was willing to believe in it. The Jews, however, fulfilled that dream and with the birth of the state of Israel they miraculously regained a nation of their own for the first time in approximately 1,900 years.

The people of Israel, in spite of centuries-long persecution and torment while having been scattered in lands not their own, held fast to their faith, culture, and language and constantly made improvements on them. After the founding of the modern state of Israel, they cultivated the barren lands and placed much emphasis on developing a variety of industries that allowed their nation to join the ranks of the developed countries, and are a remarkable people who have withstood and prospered amidst constant challenges and threats to their very survivable as a nation.

After the founding of Manmin Central Church in 1982, God has revealed to me in the inspiration of the Holy Spirit a great deal on Israel because the independence of Israel is a sign in the last days and the fulfillment of the prophecy in the Bible.

Hear the word of the LORD, O nations, And declare in the coastlands afar off, And say, "He who scattered Israel will gather him And keep him as a shepherd keeps his flock" (Jeremiah 31:10).

God has chosen the people of Israel in order to reveal His providence by which He has created and has been cultivating man. First of all, God made Abraham the "father of faith," and established Jacob, grandson of Abraham, as the founder of Israel, and God has been proclaiming His will to Jacob's descendants and accomplishing the providence of the cultivation of mankind.

When Israel believed in God's word and walked according

to His will in obedience, it enjoyed great glory and honor above all nations. When it distanced itself from God and was disobedient to Him, however, Israel was subject to a variety of torment, including foreign invasions and its people's being forced to live as vagabonds in all corners of the earth.

Even when Israel faced difficulties on account of its sins, however, God has never either forsaken or forgotten them. Israel was always bound to God through His covenant with Abraham and God never ceased working for them.

Under God's extraordinary care and guidance, Israel as a people was always preserved, achieved independence, and once again became a nation above all nations. How could the people of Israel be preserved and why was Israel restored?

Many people say, "The survival of the Jewish nation is a miracle." As the kinds and magnitude of persecution and oppression the Jewish people endured during the Diaspora exceeded any description and imagination, the history of Israel alone attests to the truthfulness of the Bible.

Yet, even a greater degree of distress and anguish than what the Jews faced will take place following the Second Advent of Jesus Christ. Of course, people who have accepted Jesus as their Savior will be lifted up into the air and partake in the Wedding Banquet with the Lord. Those who will not have accepted Jesus as their Savior, however, will not be lifted up into the air at the time of His return and will suffer the Great Tribulation for seven years.

"For behold, the day is coming, burning like a furnace; and all the arrogant and every evildoer will be chaff; and the day that is coming will set them ablaze," says the LORD of hosts, "so that it will leave them neither root nor branch" (Malachi 4:1).

God has already revealed to me in detail the calamities that are to unfold during the seven years of the Great Tribulation. For that reason, it is my earnest desire for the people of Israel God's elect to accept, without any further delay, Jesus who walked on the earth some two thousand years ago, as their Savior so that not one of them will be left behind to suffer the Great Tribulation.

On the 25th anniversary of Manmin Central Church, I have written and dedicated a work providing answers to the Jews' millennia-long thirst for the Messiah and to age-long questions that are constantly raised.

May each reader of this book take to heart God's desperate message of love and come to meet without any further delay the Messiah whom God has sent for all mankind!

I love each of you with all my heart.

February 2008
At Gethsemane Prayer House

Jaerock Lee

xii

The Author

Dr. Jaerock Lee

Dr. Jaerock Lee was born in Muan, Jeonnam Province, Republic of Korea, in 1943. In his twenties, Dr. Lee suffered from a variety of incurable diseases for seven years and awaited death with no hope for recovery. One day in the spring of 1974, however, he was led to a church by his sister and when he knelt down to pray, the living God immediately healed him of all his diseases.

From the moment Dr. Lee met the living God through that wonderful experience, he has loved God with all his heart and sincerity, and in 1978 was called to be a servant of God. He prayed fervently so that he could clearly understand the will of God and wholly accomplish it, and obeyed all the word of God. In 1982, he founded Manmin Central Church in Seoul, S. Korea, and countless works of God, including miraculous healings and wonders, have been taking place at his church.

In 1986, Dr. Lee was ordained as a pastor at the Annual Assembly of Jesus' Sungkyul Church of Korea, and four years later in 1990, his sermons began to be broadcast to Australia, Russia, the Philippines, and many more through the Far East Broadcasting Company, the Asia Broadcast Station, and the Washington Christian Radio System.

Three years later in 1993, Manmin Central Church was selected as one of the "World's Top 50 Churches" by the *Christian World* magazine (US) and he received an Honorary Doctorate of Divinity from Christian Faith College, Florida, USA, and in 1996 a Ph. D. in Ministry from Kingsway Theological Seminary, Iowa, USA.

Since 1993, Dr. Lee has taken the lead in world mission through many overseas crusades in the USA, Tanzania, Argentina, Uganda, Japan, Pakistan, Kenya, the Philippines, Honduras, India, Russia, Germany, Peru and DR Congo, and in 2002 he was called a "worldwide pastor" by major Christian newspapers in Korea for his work in various overseas crusades.

As of February 2008, Manmin Central Church is a congregation of more than 100,000 members and 7,550 domestic and overseas branch churches throughout the globe, and has so far commissioned more than 126 missionaries to 25 countries, including the United States, Russia, Germany, Canada, Japan, China, France, India, Kenya, and many more.

To this day, Dr. Lee has written 50 books, including bestsellers *Tasting Eternal Life before Death, My Life My Faith, The Way of Salvation, The Measure of Faith, Heaven I & II, Hell,* and *The Power of God,* and his works have been translated into more than 25 languages.

Dr. Lee is currently founder and president of a number of missionary organizations and associations, including Chairman, The United Holiness Church of Korea; President, The Nation Evangelization Paper; President, Manmin World Mission; Founder, Manmin TV; Founder & Board Chairman, Global Christian Network (GCN); Founder & Board Chairman, The World Christian Doctors Network (WCDN); and Founder & Board Chairman, Manmin International Seminary (MIS).

FOREWORD

I give all thanks and glory to God for guiding and blessing us to publish *Awaken, Israel!* in the last days. This work has been published in accordance with the will of God who seeks to awaken and save Israel, and is organized by the immeasurable love of God who wishes not to lose one last soul.

Chapter 1, "Israel: God's Elect," explores the reasons for God's creation and cultivation of all mankind on the earth and for His Providence by which He selected and governs the people of Israel as His elect in the history of mankind. The Chapter also introduces Israel's great forefathers as well as Our Lord, who came into this world according to the prophecy that had foretold the coming of the Savior of all peoples from the house of David.

By examining the Biblical prophecies on the Messiah, Chapter 2, "The Messiah Sent by God," testifies to Jesus' being the Messiah whose arrival Israel still eagerly awaits and how, according to the law on the redemption of the land, He satisfies all the qualifications as the Savior of mankind. Furthermore, the second Chapter investigates how Old

Testament prophecies on the Messiah have been fulfilled by Jesus and the relationship between the history of Israel and the death of Jesus.

The third Chapter, "The God in Whom Israel Believes," takes a close look at the people of Israel who strictly obey the law and its traditions, and explains to them what God is pleased with. In addition, reminding them that they have distanced themselves from the will of God because of the tradition of elders they produced, the Chapter exhorts them to fathom the true will of God for having given them the law in the first place and to fulfill the law by love.

Explored in the final Chapter "Watch and Listen!" are our time, on which the Bible has prophesied as "the end time," as well as the imminent appearance of the antichrist and the overview of the Seven-year Great Tribulation. Moreover, in testifying to the two secrets of God, which have been prepared in His infinite love for His elect so that the people of Israel might reach salvation at the final moments of the cultivation of mankind, the last Chapter entreats the people of Israel not to forsake the last opportunity of salvation.

When the first man Adam committed the sin of disobedience and was driven out from the Garden of Eden, God had him live in the land of Israel. Thenceforth, during the history of the cultivation of mankind, God has waited for millennia and is still waiting today in hopes of gaining true children.

There is no more time to delay or waste. May each of you come to realize that our time is indeed the last days and prepare to receive our Lord who is to return as the King of kings and the Lord of lords, in His name I earnestly pray!

February 2008
Geum-sun Vin, Editor-in-Chief

COMPLIMENT

"Awaken, Israel! Hear, O Israel!"

I would like to begin my recommendation of *Awaken, Israel* written by my spiritual friend Dr. Jaerock Lee with the dire words of Our Lord Jesus for the Israelites, "My heart is consumed."

Our Lord most likely had uttered those words when He had foreseen the crucifixion at Golgotha, the religious persecution in the Middle Ages, and the Holocaust during World War II.

Many prophets in the Bible had prophesied the future by God's power but their ability could not be comparable to the way in which Lord saw through the future. This is because He is the beginning and the end of the history of mankind.

I often think that the suffering of the Israelites is the repetition of the Passion of Our Lord. Like the Israelites, He was held in contempt; those who had not yet accepted Him as their Savior spat at Him, flogged Him, unfairly condemned Him, and scorned and humiliated Him at Golgotha.

"Hear, O Israel! Awaken, Israel!"

"Hear, O Israel! The LORD is our God, the LORD is one!"

I heard from heaven the following prayer: "Hear O, Israel! Our God Almighty! He is one!"

This prayer is recited by Jewish children and is also the line of prayer spiritual individuals utter to God prior to their death. It is no ordinary line of prayer; it is an expression of tremendous spiritual thirst and desperation of those who desire to draw nearer to God.

When we say "Awaken" in our prayer, we become one with the Abraham, Isaac, and Jacob, our fathers of faith who had served in God in the land of Israel long ago, and when we utter, "Awaken, Israel!" we are offering to God the fragrance of our prayer with countless angels in heaven, joining them in proclaiming, "Praise forevermore the Kingdom of Our Lord and His name!"

In this uncommon prayer, there is a quote from the Torah, which reads, "You shall love the LORD your God with all your heart and with all your soul and with all your might."

Sublime love causes one to sacrifice himself for others.

The subject of such sublime love is God the Creator, God of all mankind.

Throughout history, however, mankind's relationship with God has depended on God's showing His love for those He has created, when it has always been He who should have received our love.

The ultimate proof of God's great love for us was offered to us when His Only Begotten Son bore all sins of mankind and died on our behalf.

The Bible tells us, "Faith comes from hearing." Through the prayer above, we can believe in the love of God our

Savior.

While "Awaken, Israel!" and "Hear, O Israel!" are lines of prayer, they are also words of blessing. Following, "The LORD is our God, the LORD is one!" and the line "You shall love the LORD your God with all your heart and with all your soul and with all your might," the Jews pray, "Praise forevermore the Kingdom of Our Lord and His name," a line that is not found in the Torah. Why is that?

By acknowledging the Kingdom and the name of God who has been in existence before the ages, a concept unfathomable to man, we are affirming the prayer we utter.

Unless someone wakes us from our sleep, we will be left in spiritual slumber.

"Wake up! Wake up now! The calamity is coming and you have to be ready for it," the people of God and angels urge them. "Awake, Israel! Calamities are coming your way."

The people of Israel, however, are in such deep spiritual slumber now that they are unable to wake up. The calamity is coming.

The conscienceless enemy of calamity is approaching but Israel is blissfully asleep, unaware of the imminent arrival of the enemy.

This is why my spiritual friend Dr. Jaerock Lee, the author of this book and the lover of Israel, is calling out to God's elect today.

"Awaken, Israel!"

Dr. Jaerock Lee is a servant of God's power and guides

God's workers in love and in spirit. Dr. Lee will awaken the Israelites through this work, with his messages from the pulpit, and on television.

"Awaken, Israel! Behold your God. Trust in Him and the calamity will be destroyed and driven from your land. If we are with the Lord and He is with us, whom shall we fear? This work is God's signal for His elect. Wake up, open your eyes, and look around you. Know your friend and know your enemy. Know God's will. Many of our friends who have become our enemies now attack us. This has happened to fathers of faithfulness and is happening to us today."

People of Israel! your time has come! Can you feel the breath of your enemy filled with anger?

Just as David was awakened before his duel with Goliath, wake up. Press down the enemy with a sling and a stone.

God's elect Israel! Hear the words Jesus of Nazareth is telling each of you.

"Behold, I stand at the door and knock; if anyone hears My voice and opens the door, I will come in to him and will dine with him, and he with Me."

Never forget, people of the Torah!

Remember the One who will not back down on His promise but will faithfully keep it. Many people do not hear the words of God's prophets because they do not take to their heart the words of the One who tells them, "A new commandment I give to you, that you love one another."

It is not easy to love from the start.
Perseverance must precede love.
The root of perseverance shall bear the fruit of love.
This love is neither abstract nor romantic.

Only the love we have for God and the love in His Providence will bring us closer to the ones near us and propel them to overcome the enemy of His elect.

Let's pray like this: "God! Give the people of Israel the strength of love and a steadfast spirit. By the rams' horns of the Holy Spirit, allow them to forget the past, renew their spirit, and strengthen them so that they will partake in Your new work. Pour Your strength upon them so that they will magnify You!"

Dr. Mikhail Morguils

February 2008
Florida, U.S.A.

"Star of David," a symbol of Jewish community, on the flag of Israel

Chapter 1

ISRAEL: GOD'S ELECT

Beginning of the Cultivation of Mankind

Moses, Israel's great leader who set free its people from bondage in Egypt and led them into the Promised Land of Canaan and served as God's proxy, began His word in the Book of Genesis as follows:

"In the beginning God created the heavens and the earth" (1:1).

God created the heavens and the earth and everything in them in six days, and rested on, blessed, and sanctified the seventh day. Why, then, did God the Creator create the universe and everything therein? Why has He created man and allowed countless people since Adam to live on the earth?

God Sought Those with Whom He Could Exchange Love Eternally

Before the creation of the heavens and the earth, the almighty God existed in the limitless universe as the light in which the sound was embedded. After a long time of solitude, God desired to have those with whom He could exchange love eternally.

God possessed not only divine nature that defined Him as the Creator but also human nature by which He felt joy, anger, sorrow, and pleasure. So, He desired to give and receive love with others. In the Bible are many references that point to God's possession of human nature. He was pleased with and delighted in the righteous deeds of the Israelites (Deuteronomy 10:15; Proverbs 16:7), but grieved and became angry with them when they sinned (Exodus 32:10; Numbers 11:1, 32:13).

There are times when each individual desires to be by himself but he will become even more joyous and blissful if he has a friend with whom he can share his heart. As God possessed human nature, He desired to have those to whom He could give His love, whose heart He could fathom, and vice versa.

'Wouldn't it be joyful and touching to have children who could fathom My heart and with whom I could give and receive love in this vast yet profound realm?'

At the time of His choosing, therefore, God devised a plan to gain true children who would take after Him. Toward that end, God created not only the spiritual realm but also the physical realm in which mankind was to live.

Some may ponder, 'There are many heavenly host and angels in heaven who are nothing but obedient. Why did God go through the trouble of creating man?' Except for a few angels, however, most of heavenly beings do not possess the human nature that is the most significant of all elements required in giving and receiving love: free will by which they choose on their own. Such heavenly beings are like robots; they are obedient as commanded but without feeling joy, anger, sorrow, or pleasure, they are unable to give and receive love stemming from the depths of their heart.

Suppose there are two children and one of them, without ever expressing his emotions, opinions, or love, is obedient and does well what he is told. The other child, even though he disappoints his parents from time to time in his free will, is quick to repent of his wrongdoings, clings to his parents in love, and expresses his heart in a variety of ways.

Of these two, whom would you prefer? You will most likely choose the latter. Even if you have a robot that does all the chores for you, not one of you would prefer that robot to your own children. By the same token, God preferred man who would gladly obey Him with his reason and emotions, to robot-like heavenly host and angels.

God's Providence to Gain True Children

After creating the first man Adam, God proceeded to create the Garden of Eden and allowed him to rule over it. Everything was plentiful in the Garden of Eden and Adam ruled over all things with the free will and the authority which God gave him. However, there was one thing God forbade him.

From any tree of the garden you may eat freely; but from the tree of the knowledge of good and evil you shall not eat, for in the day that you eat from it you will surely die (Genesis 2:16-17).

This was a system that God established between God the Creator and the created mankind, and He wanted Adam to obey Him in his free will and from the depths of his heart. After a long time had passed, however, Adam failed to keep in mind God's word and committed the sin of disobedience by eating of the tree of the knowledge of good and evil.

In Genesis 3 is a scene in which the serpent, which was instigated by Satan, asked Eve, "Indeed, has God said, 'You shall not eat from any tree of the garden'?" Eve responded, "God has said, 'You shall not eat from [the tree which is in the middle of the garden] or touch it, or you will die.'"

God clearly told Eve, "In the day that you eat from it you will surely die," but she changed God's command and said, "You will die."

Upon realizing that Eve did not take God's command to her heart, the serpent became more aggressive with its temptation. "You surely will not die!" it told Eve. "For God knows that in the day you eat from it your eyes will be opened, and you will be like God, knowing good and evil."

When Satan breathed in greed through the woman's mind,

the tree of the knowledge of good and evil began to look different in her eyes. The tree looked good for food, and was a delight to the eyes, and the tree was desirable to make her wise. Eve ate its fruit and gave some to her husband, who also ate it.

This is how Adam and Eve committed the sin of disobeying God's word and surely ended up facing death (Genesis 2:17).

Here, "death" refers not to the fleshly death in which the breathing ceases in a human body but to spiritual death. After eating from the tree of the knowledge of good and evil, Adam gave birth to children and died at the age of 930 (Genesis 5:2-5). From this alone we know that "death" here does not refer to physical death.

Man was originally created as a blend of spirit, soul, and body. He possessed spirit through which he could communicate with God; soul that was under the control of the spirit; and the body that served as a shield for both the spirit and the soul. On account of forsaking God's command and committing a sin, the spirit died and its communication with God was also severed, and this is the "death" of which God spoke in Genesis 2:17.

After their sinning, Adam and Eve were driven out from the beautiful and plentiful Garden of Eden. Thus began the torment for all mankind. The pain in childbirth was greatly multiplied for the woman who was to now desire her husband and be ruled by him, while the man was to eat of the cursed ground in toil all the days of his life (Genesis 3:16-17).

On this Genesis 3:23 tells us, *"Therefore the LORD God sent him out from the garden of Eden, to cultivate the ground from which he was taken."* Here, "cultivate the ground" signifies not only the man's toiling to eat of the ground but to the fact that he – formed of dust from the ground – was also to "cultivate his heart" while living on the earth.

Cultivation of Mankind Begins with Adam's Sinning

Adam was created as a living being and had no evil in his heart, so he did not have to cultivate his heart. After his sinning, however, Adam's heart was smeared with untruth and then he needed to cultivate his heart into a clean heart as it had been before his sinning.

Thus, Adam had to cultivate his heart that had become corrupt by untruths and sins into clean heart and come forth as a true child of God after he sinned. When the Bible says, "God sent him out from the garden of Eden, to cultivate the ground from which he was taken," it means this, and it is referred to as "God's cultivation of mankind."

Conventionally, "cultivation" refers to a procedure in which a farmer sows seeds, takes care of his crops, and reaps the fruit. In order to "cultivate" mankind on the earth and gain the good fruit that means "true children of God," God

8

sowed the first seeds, Adam and Eve. Through Adam and Eve who disobeyed God, countless children have been born and through God's cultivation of mankind, countless have been born again as God's children by cultivating their hearts and recovering the lost image of God.

Thus, "God's cultivation of mankind" refers to the entire process in which God takes charge of and governs the history of mankind, from their creation to the Judgment, in order to gain His true children.

Just as a farmer overcomes floods, droughts, frosts, hails, and the vermin after first sowing seeds but reaps beautiful and delightful fruit in the end, God has been controlling everything to gain true children who come forth after undergoing death, disease, parting, and other types of sufferings during their lives in this world.

The Reason God Placed the Tree of the Knowledge of Good and Evil in the Garden of Eden

Some people ask, "Why did God place the tree of the knowledge of good and evil through which man came to sin and was led to destruction?" The reason that God placed the tree of the knowledge of good and evil, however, is because of God's wonderful providence by which He would lead men to become aware of 'relativity.'

Most people assume that Adam and Eve were nothing but happy to live in the Garden of Eden because there were no tears, grief, disease, or torment in the Garden. But Adam and Eve did not know true happiness and love because they had no idea of relativity in the Garden of Eden.

For instance, how would two children react to receiving the same toy if one child has been born into and raised in an affluent family and the other in a family in need? The latter child would be more grateful and joyful from the depths of his heart than the child with an affluent background.

If you understand the true worth of something, you have to know and experience the complete opposite of it. Only when you have suffered from disease, will you be able to appreciate the true value of good health. Only when you have become aware of death and hell, will you be able to appreciate the value of eternal life and thank the God of love from your heart for giving you the eternal heaven.

In the plentiful Garden of Eden, the first man Adam enjoyed everything that God had given him, even the authority to rule over every other creature. However, as they were not the fruit of his toil and sweat, Adam was unable to fully grasp their importance or appreciate God for them. Only after Adam was driven out into this world and experienced tears, sorrow, diseases, torment, misfortune, and death did he come to realize the difference between joy and grief and how valuable freedom and prosperity God had given in the Garden of Eden.

What good would eternal life do for us if we did not know

joy or sorrow? Even though we face difficulties for a little while, if we can later realize and say, "This is joy!" our lives will become all the more worthwhile and blessed.

Aren't there any parents who would not send their children to school but have them stay at home simply because they know studying is difficult? If the parents truly love their children, they will send their children to school and lead them to study difficult matters diligently and to experience various things so that they will build a better future.

The heart of God, who created mankind and has been cultivating them, is exactly the same. For that very reason, God placed the tree of the knowledge of good and evil, did not prevent Adam from eating of the tree in his free will, and allowed him to experience joy, anger, sorrow, and pleasure during the course of the cultivation of mankind. This is because man can love and worship God, who Himself is love and the truth, from the depths of his heart only after he has experienced relativity and fathomed true love, joy, and gratitude.

Through the process of human cultivation, God wanted to gain true children who have come to know His heart and taken after it, and to live with them in heaven sharing eternal and true love with them forever.

The Cultivation of Mankind Begins in Israel

When the first man Adam was driven out from the Garden

of Eden after disobeying God's word, he was not given the right to choose the land where he was to settle but instead God designated an area for him. That area was Israel.

In this was embedded God's will and providence. After harboring a grand plan of the cultivation of mankind, God selected the people of Israel as a model of the cultivation of mankind. For that reason God specifically allowed for Adam to live a new life in a land where the nation of Israel was to be built.

After time passed, countless nations came from Adam's descendants and the nation of Israel was built by the time of Jacob, a descendant of Abraham. God desired to reveal His glory and His providence of cultivating mankind through the history of Israel. It was not only to the Israelites but to people all over the world. Therefore, the history of Israel of which God has Himself been taken charge of is not merely a history of a people but a divine message for all mankind.

Why, then, did God select Israel as the model of the cultivation of mankind? That was because of their superior character, in other words, their excellent innermost being.

Israel is a descendant of the 'father of faith' Abraham in whom God was well-pleased, and also a descendant of Jacob who was so tenacious that he strove with God and prevailed. This is why, even after losing their homeland and living a life of vagabonds for centuries, the people of Israel did not lose their identity.

Above all, the people of Israel have preserved, for thousands of years, God's word that have been prophesied through men of God and have lived by it. Of course, there have been times in which the whole nation distanced itself from God's word and sinned against Him but eventually its people repented and returned to God. They have never lost their faith in their LORD God.

The restoration of an independent Israel in the 20th century clearly shows the kind of heart that its people has as Jacob's descendants.

Ezekiel 38:8 tells us, *"After many days you will be summoned; in the latter years you will come into the land that is restored from the sword, whose inhabitants have been gathered from many nations to the mountains of Israel which had been a continual waste; but its people were brought out from the nations, and they are living securely, all of them."* Here, "the latter years" refer to the end time when the cultivation of mankind will draw to its close and "the mountains of Israel" signify the city of Jerusalem, seated nearly 760 m (2,592 feet) above the sea level.

Therefore, when Prophet Ezekiel says that many *"inhabitants [will] have been gathered from many nations to the mountains of Israel,"* it meant that the Israelis would gather from across the world and restore the state of Israel. According this word of God, Israel, which had been destroyed by the Romans in 70 A.D., declared its statehood on May 14,

1948. The land had been nothing but "a continual waste" but today, Israelis built a strong nation that no others can easily overlook or challenge.

The Purpose of God's Having Selected the Israelites

Why did God begin the cultivation of mankind in the land of Israel? Why did God select the people of Israel, and govern the history of Israel?

First, God willed to proclaim to all nations through the history of Israel that He is the Creator of the heavens and the earth, that He alone is the true God, and that He is alive. Through the studying of the history of Israel, even the Gentiles can easily feel the presence of God and fathom His providence to govern the history of mankind.

So all the peoples of the earth will see that you are called by the name of the LORD, and they will be afraid of you (Deuteronomy 28:10).

Blessed are you, O Israel; Who is like you, a people saved by the LORD, Who is the shield of your help And the sword of your majesty! So your enemies will cringe before you, And you will tread upon their high places (Deuteronomy 33:29).

God's elect, Israel has enjoyed a great privilege, and we can easily find it from the history of Isarel.

For example, when Rahab received two men Joshua had sent to spy the land of Canaan, she said to them, *"We have heard how the LORD dried up the water of the Red Sea before you when you came out of Egypt, and what you did to the two kings of the Amorites who were beyond the Jordan, to Sihon and Og, whom you utterly destroyed. When we heard it, our hearts melted and no courage remained in any man any longer because of you; for the LORD your God, He is God in heaven above and on earth beneath"* (Joshua 2:9-11).

During the Israelites' captivity in Babylon, Daniel walked with God and Nebuchadnezzar King of Babylon experienced God with whom Daniel walked. After the king experienced God, he could only *"praise, exalt and honor the King of heaven, for all His works are true and His ways just, and He is able to humble those who walk in pride"* (Daniel 4:37).

The same thing happened while Israel was under the reign of Persia. Upon seeing the living God at work and responding to the prayer of Queen Esther, *"many among the peoples of the land became Jews, for the dread of the Jews had fallen on them"* (Esther 8:17).

Thus, when even the Gentiles experienced the living God who worked for the Israelites, they came to fear and worship

God. And even the posterity we come to know of the majesty of God and worship Him from such events and instances.

Second, God selected Israel and guided its people because He wanted all mankind to realize through the history of Israel the reason that He created men and has been cultivating them.

God cultivates mankind because He seeks to gain true children. A true child of God is the one who has taken after God who is goodness and love in essence, and who is righteous and holy. It is because such children of God love Him and live by His will.

When Israel lived by God's commandments and served Him, He set the Israelites above all peoples and nations. On the contrary, when the people of Israel served idols and were quick to forsake God's commandments, they were subject to all kinds of torment and such calamities as war and natural disasters or even captivity.

Through each step of the process, the Israelites learned to humble themselves before God, and each time they humbled themselves, God restored them with His unfailing mercy and love and brought them into the arms of His grace.

When King Solomon loved God and kept His commandments, he enjoyed great glory and splendor but when the king began to distance himself from God and serve idols, the glory and splendor he enjoyed waned. When the kings of Israel such as David, Jehoshaphat, and Hezekiah walked in the law of God, the country was powerful and thrived, but it was weak and subject to foreign invasions during the reigns of kings who shunned God's ways.

The history of Israel plainly reveals God's will this way and serves as a mirror that reflects God's will to all peoples and nations. His will proclaims that when people formed in God's image and likeness keep His commandments and become sanctified according to His word, they will receive God's blessings and live in His favor.

Israel was selected to reveal God's providence among all nations and peoples, and has received a tremendous blessing through serving Him as the nation of priests in charge of God's word. Even when its people sinned, God forgave them of their sins and restored them as long as they repented with a humble heart, just as He had promised their great forefathers.

Above all, the greatest blessing that God promised and set aside for His elect was the marvelous promise of glory that the Messiah was to come among them.

Great Forefathers

Throughout the long history of mankind, God has protected Israel in His wings and sent men of God at His destined time so that the name of Israel might not disappear. The men of God were the ones who came forth as the proper fruits in accordance with the providence of God's cultivation of mankind and abided in the word of God with the love for Him. God laid the foundation of the nation of Israel through great forefathers of Israel.

Abraham, the Father of Faith

Abraham was marked as the father of faith by his faith and obedience, and was to bring forth a great nation. He was born some four thousand years ago in Ur of the Chaldeans, and after he was called by God he won God's love and recognition to the point of being called as God's "friend."

God called on Abraham and made him the following promise:

> "Go forth from your country, And from your relatives And from your father's house, To the land

which I will show you; And I will make you a great nation, And I will bless you, And make your name great; And so you shall be a blessing" (Genesis 12:1-2).

At the time, Abraham was no longer a young man, lacked an heir, and had no idea to where he was going; therefore, it was not the easiest of things to obey. Even though he did not know where he was headed, Abraham went forth because he trusted only and wholly in the word of God who never breaks His promises at all. Thus, Abraham walked by faith in everything he did, and during the course of his life he received all the blessings that God had promised.

Abraham did not show God just perfect obedience and deeds of faith but always pursued goodness and peace with the people around him.

For example, when Abraham left Haran according to God's command, his nephew Lot came with him. When their possessions became great, Abraham and Lot were no longer able to remain in the same land. The insufficiency of pastures and water led to "strife between the herdsmen of Abram's livestock and the herdsmen of Lot's livestock" (Genesis 13:7). Even though Abraham was much older, he did not seek or insist on his benefits. He conceded to his nephew Lot in selecting the better land. He said to Lot in Genesis 13:9, *"Is not the whole land before you? Please separate from me; if to the left, then I will go to the right; or if to the right, then I will go to the left."*

And because Abraham was a man of clean heart, he did not take a thread or a sandal thong or anything that was others' (Genesis 14:23). When God told him that the cities of Sodom and Gomorrah drenched in sin would be destroyed, Abraham, a man of spiritual love, pleaded with God and received His word that He would not destroy Sodom if there were ten righteous men found in the city.

The goodness and faith of Abraham were perfect to the point of his obeying God's command that now called for the life of his one and only son as a burnt offering.

In Genesis 22:2, God commanded Abraham, *"Take now your son, your only son, whom you love, Isaac, and go to the land of Moriah, and offer him there as a burnt offering on one of the mountains of which I will tell you."*

Isaac was a son born to Abraham when Abraham was one hundred years old. Before Isaac was born, God already told Abraham that the one who would come forth from his own body should be his heir and that the number of his descendants would equal the numbers of stars. Had Abraham followed fleshly thoughts, he would not have been able to comply with the commandment of God and to offer Isaac. Yet, Abraham obeyed immediately without asking for any reasons.

The moment when Abraham stretched out his hand to slay Isaac after building the altar, the angel of God called to him and said, *"Abraham, Abraham! Do not stretch out your hand against the lad, and do nothing to him; for now I know that you fear God, since you have not withheld your son, your only son, from Me."* How blessed and touching a scene is this?

As he never relied on his fleshly thoughts, there were no conflicts or anxiety within Abraham's heart and he could only obey the command of God by faith. He placed his whole trust in the faithful God who surely fulfills whatever He has promised, the almighty God who revives the dead, and the God of love who desires to give His children only good things. As Abraham's heart was only of obedience and even showed the deed of faith, God accepted Abraham as the father of faith.

Because you have done this thing and have not withheld your son, your only son, indeed I will greatly bless you, and I will greatly multiply your seed as the stars of the heavens and as the sand which is on the seashore; and your seed shall possess the gate of their enemies. In your seed all the nations of the earth shall be blessed, because you have obeyed My voice (Genesis 22:16-18).

As Abraham possessed the kind and magnitude of goodness and faith to please God, he was called the "friend" of God and deemed the father of faith. Also, he became the father of all nations and the source of all blessings just as God promised him when He first called on him, *"And I will bless those who bless you, And the one who curses you I will curse And in you all the families of the earth will be blessed"* (Genesis 12:3).

God's Providence through Jacob, the Father of Israel, and Joseph the Dreamer

Isaac was born to Abraham the father of faith and the two sons Esau and Jacob were born to Isaac. God selected Jacob, whose heart was superior to that of his brother, when he was yet in his mother's womb. Jacob would later be called "Israel" and become the origin of the nation of Israel and the father of the Twelve Tribes.

To the extent of purchasing his older brother Esau's birthright for lentil stew and snatching away his brother Esau's blessings by deceiving his father Isaac, Jacob eagerly desired blessings of God and spiritual matters. Jacob had deceitful traits within himself but God knew that once Jacob was transformed, he would become a great vessel. For that reason, God allowed Jacob twenty years of trial so that his self might be completely broken and he might be humbled.

When Jacob snatched away the birthright of his older brother Esau in a crafty way, Esau tried to kill him and Jacob had to flee away from him. After all, Jacob came to live at his uncle Laban's and pasture sheep and goats. He had to toil in taking care of his uncle's sheep and goats. So, he confessed in Genesis 31:40, *"By day the heat consumed me and the frost by night, and my sleep fled from my eyes."*

God pays back each individual according to what he sows. He saw Jacob doing that faithfully, and blessed him with great wealth. When God told him to return to his homeland, Jacob left Laban's and set out for home with his family and possessions. Upon reaching the Jabbok River, Jacob heard that his brother Esau was on the other side river with 400 men.

Jacob could not return to Laban's because of the promise he made with his uncle. Nor could he go cross the river and go forward towards Esau who was burning with revenge. Finding himself in a predicament, Jacob no longer relied on his wisdom but committed everything to God in prayer. Completely ridding himself of every frame of his thoughts, Jacob earnestly petitioned with God in prayer to the point of dislocating his thigh.

Jacob struggled with God and prevailed, so God blessed him saying, *"Your name shall no longer be Jacob, but Israel; for you have striven with God and with men and have prevailed"* (Genesis 32:28). Then Jacob could be reconciled to his brother Esau as well.

The reason that God selected Jacob was because he was so persistent and upright that through trials, he would be able to become a great vessel to play a significant role in the history of Israel.

Jacob had 12 sons and the 12 sons laid the foundations to form the nation of Israel. However, because they were still a mere tribe, God planned to place them within the boundaries of Egypt, which was a powerful country, until the descendants of Jacob could become a great nation.

This plan was of the love of God who was to protect them from other nations. The person who was entrusted with this monumental task was Joseph who was the 11th son of Jacob.

Among his 12 sons, Jacob was so remarkably partial towards Joseph that he clothed him with the varicolored tunic and so forth. Joseph became the target of his brothers' hatred and jealousy and was sold to slavery in Egypt at the age of 17 by his brothers. But he never complained or held his brothers in contempt.

Joseph was sold to the house of Potiphar, Pharaoh's officer, the captain of the bodyguard. There he worked diligently and faithfully and won the favor and trust of Potiphar. Therefore, Joseph became an overseer over Potiphar's house and was entrusted with everything in the household.

A problem arose, though. Joseph was handsome in form and appearance and his master's wife began to seduce him. Joseph was upright and sincerely feared God, so when she seduced him, he boldly said to her, *"How could I do this great evil and sin against God?"* (Genesis 39:9)

After all, at her unreasonable accusations, Joseph was imprisoned where the king's prisoners were confined. Even in the prison, God was with Joseph, and with God's favor on his side, Joseph was soon in charge of "whatever was done" in the prison.

From such steps along the way, Joseph was able to gain wisdom by which he could later run a nation, cultivate his political dispositions, and become a great vessel who could embrace many people in his heart.

After interpreting the Pharaoh's dreams and even offering wise solutions to the problem that the Pharaoh and his people would have to meet with, Joseph became the ruler of Egypt after the Pharaoh. Thus, by God's profound providence and through those trials given to Joseph, God placed Joseph at the post of viceroy at the age of 30 in one of the most powerful nations at that time.

Just as Joseph predicted Pharaoh's dreams, seven years of famine struck the Near East including Egypt and, as he already made preparations for such an event, Joseph could deliver all Egyptians. Joseph's brothers came to Egypt in search of food, reunited with their brother and the rest of the family soon relocated to Egypt in which they lived in prosperity and paved the way to give birth to the nation of Israel.

Moses: A Great Leader who Made the Exodus a Reality

After settling down in Egypt, Israel's descendants grew in number and in prosperity and soon became great and numerous enough to form a nation of their own.

When a new king, who did not know Joseph, came to power, he began to guard against the prosperity and strength of

Israel's descendants. The king and court officials soon began making the Israelites' lives bitter with hard labor in mortar and bricks and at all kinds of labor in the field, all their labors which they rigorously imposed on them (Exodus 1:13-14).

However, *"the more they afflicted [the Israelites], the more they multiplied and the more they spread out."* Pharaoh soon ordered all Israel's boys to be killed upon birth. Upon hearing the Israelites' cry for help because of their bondage, God remembered His covenant with Abraham, Isaac, and Jacob.

> *I will give to you and to your descendants after you, the land of your sojournings, all the land of Canaan, for an everlasting possession; and I will be their God (Genesis 17:8).*

> *The land which I gave to Abraham and Isaac, I will give it to you, And I will give the land to your descendants after you (Genesis 35:12).*

In order to lead the sons of Israel out of their torment and bring them into the land of Canaan, God prepared a man who would obey His commands unconditionally and guide His people with His heart.

That individual was Moses. His parents hid Moses for three months after his birth, but when they could no longer hide him, they put him into a wicker basket and placed the basket among the reeds by the bank of the Nile. When the daughter of Pharaoh discovered the child in that wicker basket and decided to keep him as her own, the baby's sister who stood at a distance to find out what would happen to the baby recommended to the daughter of the Pharaoh Moses' biological mother as a nurse.

Thus, Moses was raised at the royal palace and by his biological mother, so he grew up naturally learning about God and the Israelites, his own people.

Then one day, he saw his fellow Hebrew getting beaten up by an Egyptian, and in anguish he ended up killing the Egyptian. When this was made known, Moses fled from the presence of Pharaoh and settled in the land of Midian. He pastured sheep for 40 years, and this was a part of the providence of God who sought to try and train Moses as the leader of the Exodus.

At the time of God's choosing, He called on Moses and commanded him to lead the Israelites out of Egypt and into Canaan, a land flowing with milk and honey.

As the Pharaoh had a hardened heart, he did not listen to the command of God given through Moses. As a result, God brought forth the Ten Plagues upon Egypt and forcefully brought the Israelites out of the land of Egypt.

Only after suffering the death of their firstborn sons did Pharaoh and his people kneel before God and could the people of Israel be set free from the bondage. God Himself guided the Israelites each step of their way; God parted the Red Sea so that they would cross it on dry land. When they had no water to drink, God let water spring out of a rock and when they had no food to eat, God sent forth the manna and quails. God performed these miracles and wonders through Moses to ensure the survival of millions of Israelites in the wilderness for 40 years.

The faithful God led the people of Israel into the land of Canaan through Joshua, Moses' successor. God helped Joshua and his people to cross the Jordan River by God's way and allowed them the conquest of the city of Jericho. And in His own ways, God permitted them to conquer and possess most of the land of Canaan flowing with milk and honey.

Of course, the conquest of Canaan was not only God's blessing for the Israelites but was also the result of His righteous judgment against the inhabitants of Canaan who became corrupt in sin and evil. The inhabitants of the land of Canaan became grossly corrupt and were forced to be subject to judgment, and then in His justice God led the Israelites to take the land.

As God told Abraham, *"Then in the fourth generation they will return here"* (Genesis 15:16), Abraham's descendants Jacob and his sons left Canaan for Egypt, settled there, and their descendants returned to the land of Canaan.

David Establishes a Potent Israel

After the conquest of the land of Canaan, God ruled over Israel through judges during the Period of the Judges and then, Israel became a kingdom. By the reign of King David who loved God above all else, the foundations as a nation were established.

In his youth, David killed a great Philistine warrior with a sling and a stone and in recognition of his service on the battlefield David was set over the men of war in King Saul's army. When David returned home after defeating the Philistines, many women sang as they played, and said, "Saul has slain his thousands, and David his ten thousands." And all the Israelites began to love David. King Saul plotted schemes to kill David out of jealousy.

Amidst Saul's desperate pursuits, David had two opportunities to kill the king but refused to kill the king who had been anointed by God Himself. He only did good towards the king. On one occasion, David bowed with his face to the ground, prostrated himself, and said to King Saul, *"Now, my father, see! Indeed, see the edge of your robe in my hand! For in that I cut off the edge of your robe and did not kill you, know and perceive that there is no evil or rebellion in my hands, and I have not sinned against you, though you are lying in wait for my life to take it"* (1 Samuel 24:11).

David, a man after God's own heart, pursued goodness in all things even after he became king. During his reign, David ruled his kingdom with justice and strengthened the kingdom. As God walked with the king, David was victorious in his wars against the neighboring Philistines, the Moabites, the Amalekites, the Ammonites, and the Edomites. He expanded Israel's territories and the spoils of war and tributes only increased the treasury of David's kingdom. Accordingly, he enjoyed the period of prosperity.

David also moved God's Ark of the Covenant to Jerusalem, set up the procedures for offering sacrifices, and strengthened the faith in the LORD God. The king also founded Jerusalem as the political and religious center of the kingdom and made all preparations for the Holy Temple of God to be built during the reign of his son King Solomon. .

Throughout its entire history, Israel was the most powerful and splendid during the rule of King David, and King David was greatly admired by his people and gave great glory to God. On top of all this, how great a forefather was David that the Messiah was to come from his descendants?

Elijah Brings the Israelites' Hearts Back to God

King David's son Solomon worshiped idols in his late days and the kingdom was split in half after his death. Among the 12 Tribes of Israel, ten formed the Kingdom of Israel in the north while the other remaining tribes formed the Kingdom of Judah in the south.

In the Kingdom of Israel, Prophets Amos and Hosea revealed God's will to His people while Prophets Isaiah and Jeremiah carried out the ministries in the Kingdom of Judah. Whenever the time of His choosing came, God sent His prophets and accomplished His will through them. One of them was Prophet Elijah. Elijah carried out his ministry during the reign of King Ahab in the northern kingdom.

In Elijah's time, the Gentile queen Jezebel brought Baal into Israel and idol worshipping was rampant throughout the kingdom. The first mission that Prophet Elijah had to perform was to tell King Ahab that there would be no rain in Israel for three and a half years as the result of God's judgment for their idol worshipping.

When the prophet was told that the king and the queen were trying to kill him, Elijah fled to Zarephath, which belonged to Sidon. He was provided with a morsel of bread from a widow there, and in return for her service Elijah manifested the marvelous blessings upon the widow and her bowl of flour was not exhausted nor did the jar of oil become empty until the famine came to an close. Later, Elijah also revived the dead son of the widow.

Atop Mount Carmel, Elijah battled against 450 prophets of Baal and 400 prophets of the Asherah and brought down God's fire from heaven. In order to turn the hearts of the Israelites away from idols and lead them back to God, Elijah repaired the altar of God, poured water over the offerings and the altar, and earnestly prayed to God.

"O LORD, the God of Abraham, Isaac and Israel, today let it be known that You are God in Israel and that I am Your servant and I have done all these things at Your word. Answer me, O LORD, answer me, that this people may know that You, O LORD, are God, and that You have turned their heart back again." Then the fire of the LORD fell and consumed the burnt offering and the wood and the stones and the dust, and licked up the water that was in the trench. When all the people saw it, they fell on their faces; and they said, "The LORD, He is God; the LORD, He is God." Then Elijah said to them, "Seize the prophets of Baal; do not let one of them escape." So they seized them; and Elijah brought them down to the brook Kishon, and slew them there (1 Kings 18:36-39).

In addition, he brought down rain from heaven after three and a half years of drought, crossed the Jordan River as if he were walking on dry land and prophesied on the things that were to take place. By manifesting God's wondrous power, Elijah testified to the living God clearly.

2 Kings 2:11 reads, *"As [Elijah and Elisha] were going along and talking, behold, there appeared a chariot of fire and horses of fire which separated the two of them. And Elijah*

went up by a whirlwind to heaven." Because Elijah pleased God by his faith to the utmost degree and received His love and recognition, the Prophet ascended into heaven without facing death.

Daniel Reveals God's Glory to the Nations

Two hundred and fifty years later, circa 605 B.C., in the third year of King Jehoiakim's reign, Jerusalem fell by the invasion of King Nebuchadnezzar of Babylon and many of the royal family in the Kingdom of Judah were taken captives.

As part of Nebuchadnezzar's reconciliation policy, the king ordered Ashpenaz, the chief of his officials, to bring in some of the sons of Israel, including some of the royal family and of the nobles, youths in whom was no defect, who were good-looking, showing intelligence in every branch of wisdom, endowed with understanding and discerning knowledge, and who had ability for serving in the king's court. And the king ordered him to teach them the literature and language of the Chaldeans and among such youths was Daniel (Daniel 1:3-4).

However, Daniel made up his mind that he would not defile himself with the king's choice food or with the wine which he drank. So, he sought permission from the commander of the officials that he might not defile himself (Daniel 1:8).

Even though he was a prisoner of war, Daniel received God's blessings as he feared Him in every affair of his life. God gave Daniel and his friends knowledge and intelligence in every branch of literature and wisdom. Daniel even understood all kinds of visions and dreams (Daniel 1:17).

That's why he continued gaining favor and recognition from the kings even though the kingdoms changed. Recognizing Daniel's extraordinary spirit, King Darius of Persia sought to appoint him over the entire kingdom. Then a group of court officials became jealous of Daniel and began looking for a ground of accusation against Daniel in regard to government affairs. But they could find no ground of accusation or evidence of corruption.

When they learned that Daniel prayed to God three times a day, the commissioners and satraps came before the king and urged him to create a statute that anyone who would make a petition to any god or man besides the king for a month was to be cast into the lions' den. Daniel did not waver; even at the risk of losing his reputation, high position, and his life in a lions' den, he continued praying, facing Jerusalem, as he had previously done.

By the order of the king, Daniel was thrown into the lions' den but because God sent His angel and shut the lions' mouths, Daniel was left unharmed. Upon learning this, King Darius wrote to all the peoples, nations and men of every language who were living in all the lands and let them sing praises and give glory to God:

I make a decree that in all the dominion of my
kingdom men are to fear and tremble before the God

of Daniel; For He is the living God and enduring forever, And His kingdom is one which will not be destroyed, And His dominion will be forever. He delivers and rescues and performs signs and wonders In heaven and on earth, Who has also delivered Daniel from the power of the lions (Daniel 6:26-27).

In addition to the forefathers of faith who had great renown in God mentioned above, no amount of paper and ink would suffice to describe the deeds of faith of Gideon, Barak, Samson, Jephthah, Samuel, Isaiah, Jeremiah, Ezekiel, Daniel's three friends, Esther, and all the prophets introduced in the Bible.

Great Forefathers for All the Nations of the Earth

From the earliest days of the nation of Israel, God personally charted and steered the course of its history. Each time Israel found itself in crises, God delivered them through the prophets whom He prepared, and directed the history of Israel.

Therefore, unlike that of any other nations, the history of Israel has been unfolding according to the providence of God from the days of Abraham and will continue to unfold in accordance with the plan of God until the end of the ages.

For God to appoint and use the fathers of faith among the people of Israel for His providence and plan was not only for

His elect, the Israelites but also for all peoples everywhere who have faith in God.

Abraham will surely become a great and mighty nation, and in him all the nations of the earth will be blessed (Genesis 18:18).

God desires "all the nations of the earth," to become Abraham's children by faith and to receive Abraham's blessings. He has not reserved the blessings only for His elect the Israelites. God promised Abraham in Genesis 17:4-5 that he would become the father of a multitude of nations, and in Genesis 12:3 that all the families of the earth would be blessed in him and in Genesis 22:17-18 that all the nations of the earth would be blessed in his seed.

Moreover, through the history of Israel, God has opened the path by which all the nations of the earth would come to know that only the LORD God is the true God, serve Him, and become His true children who love Him.

I permitted Myself to be sought by those who did not ask for Me; I permitted Myself to be found by those who did not seek Me. I said, 'Here am I, here am I,' To a nation which did not call on My name (Isaiah 65:1).

God established great forefathers and has personally guided

and governed the history of Israel in order to allow both the Gentiles and His elect the Israelites to call on His name. God had accomplished the history of the cultivation of mankind until then, but now He devised another marvelous plan so that He would apply the providence of human cultivation to the gentiles as well. That's why when the time of His choosing came God sent His Son into the land of Israel not just as the Messiah of Israel but as the Messiah of all mankind.

People Who Testify to Jesus Christ

Throughout the history of the cultivation of mankind, Israel was always at the center in the fulfillment of God's providence. God revealed Himself to the fathers of faith, promised them the things to take place, and fulfilled them just as He promised. He also told the Israelites that the Messiah would come from the tribe of Judah and the house of David and would save all the nations on the earth.

Therefore, Israel has waited for the Messiah who has been prophesied in the Old Testament. *The Messiah is Jesus Christ.* Of course, the people who have the faith in Judaism do not recognize Jesus as the Son of God and the Messiah, but instead they are still waiting for His coming.

However, the Messiah for whom Israel waits and the Messiah about whom the rest of this Chapter will be written is one and the same.

What do people say of Jesus Christ? If you examine the prophecies on the Messiah and their fulfillment, and the qualifications for the Messiah, you will only affirm the fact that the Messiah for whom Israel has been longing is none other than Jesus Christ.

Paul, Persecutor of Jesus Christ Turns into His Apostle

Paul was born in Tarsus, Cilicia, in modern-day Turkey, approximately 2,000 years ago, and his birth name was Saul. Saul was circumcised on the eighth day after birth, of the nation of Israel, of the tribe of Benjamin, and a Hebrew of Hebrews. Saul was found blameless as to the righteousness which is in the Law. He was also educated under Gamaliel, a teacher of the Law who was respected by all the people. He lived strictly according to the law of his fathers and had the citizenship of the Roman Empire that was the most powerful country in the world at the time. In a word, there was nothing Saul lacked in fleshly terms as far as his family, lineage, knowledge, wealth, or authority was concerned.

Because he loved God above all else, Saul zealously persecuted the followers of Jesus Christ. It was because when he heard Christians claim that the crucified Jesus was the Son of God and the Savior and that Jesus was resurrected on the third day of His burial, Saul considered it equivalent to blaspheming against God Himself.

Saul also thought that the followers of Jesus Christ posed a threat to the Pharisaic Judaism that he passionately followed. For that reason, Saul relentlessly persecuted and destroyed the church and took the lead in capturing the believers of Jesus Christ.

He imprisoned many Christians and cast votes against them when they were killed. He also punished the believers in all the synagogues, tried to force them to blaspheme against Jesus Christ there, and kept pursuing them even to foreign cities.

Then Saul underwent a remarkable experience by which his life was turned upside-down. On his way to Damascus, suddenly a light from heaven flashed around him.

"Saul, Saul, why are you persecuting Me?"
"Who are You, Lord?"
"I am Jesus whom you are persecuting."

Saul got up from the ground, but he could see nothing; the people brought him into Damascus. He stayed there three days without sight. He neither ate nor drank. After this incident, the Lord appeared in a vision to a disciple named Ananias.

Get up and go to the street called Straight, and inquire at the house of Judas for a man from Tarsus named Saul, for he is praying, and he has seen in a vision a man named Ananias come in and lay his hands on him, so that he might regain his sight ... Go, for he is a chosen instrument of Mine, to bear My name before the Gentiles and kings and the sons of Israel; for I will show him how much he must suffer for My name's sake (Acts 9:11-12; 15-16).

When Ananias laid his hand and prayed for Saul,

immediately there fell from his eyes something like scales and he regained his sight. After meeting the Lord, Saul came to realize his sins through and through, and renamed himself "Paul," which means "a small man." From that point on, Paul boldly preached to the Gentiles the living God and the gospel of Jesus Christ.

For I would have you know, brethren, that the gospel which was preached by me is not according to man. For I neither received it from man, nor was I taught it, but I received it through a revelation of Jesus Christ. For you have heard of my former manner of life in Judaism, how I used to persecute the church of God beyond measure and tried to destroy it; and I was advancing in Judaism beyond many of my contemporaries among my countrymen, being more extremely zealous for my ancestral traditions. But when God, who had set me apart even from my mother's womb and called me through His grace, was pleased to reveal His Son in me so that I might preach Him among the Gentiles, I did not immediately consult with flesh and blood, nor did I go up to Jerusalem to those who were apostles before me; but I went away to Arabia, and returned once more to Damascus (Galatians 1:11-17).

Even after meeting the Lord Jesus Christ and preaching

the gospel, Paul endured all kinds of sufferings that cannot be adequately described with words. Paul often found himself in far more labors, in far more imprisonments, beaten times without number, often in danger of death, through many sleepless nights, in hunger and thirst, often without food, in cold and exposure (2 Corinthians 11:23-27).

He could have easily lived a prosperous and comfortable life with his status, authority, knowledge, and wisdom but Paul gave all of them up and surrendered everything he had only to the Lord.

> *For I am the least of the apostles, and not fit to be called an apostle, because I persecuted the church of God. But by the grace of God I am what I am, and His grace toward me did not prove vain; but I labored even more than all of them, yet not I, but the grace of God with me (1 Corinthians 15:9-10).*

Paul could make this bold confession because he had a very vivid experience of meeting with Jesus Christ. The Lord did not just meet Paul on the road to Damascus but also affirmed His presence with Paul by manifesting marvelous works of power.

God performed extraordinary miracles by the hands of Paul, so that handkerchiefs or aprons were even carried from his body to the sick, and the diseases left them and the evil spirits went out. Paul also brought a young man named

Eutychus back to life when he fell down from the third floor and was picked up dead. Bringing a dead person back to life is not possible without the power of God.

The Old Testament mentions that Prophet Elijah brought the dead son of a widow in Zarephath back to life and Prophet Elisha revived a boy of a prominent woman in Shunem. As the Psalmist wrote in Psalm 62:11, *"Once God has spoken; Twice I have heard this: That power belongs to God,"* the power of God is given to men of God.

During his three mission trips, Paul established the foundation for the gospel of Jesus Christ to be preached to all nations by building churches at many places in Asia and Europe including Asia Minor and Greece. Thus, the path was opened through which the gospel of Jesus Christ would be preached to every corner of the earth and a myriad of souls would be saved.

Peter Manifests Great Power and Saves Countless Souls

What can we say of Peter who spearheaded the effort to preach the gospel to the Jews? He was an ordinary fisherman before he met Jesus, but after he was called on by Jesus and witnessed firsthand marvelous things Jesus did, Peter became one of His best disciples.

When Peter witnessed Jesus manifest the kind and magnitude of power that no other man could even imitate, including opening the eyes of the blind, standing up of the crippled, reviving of the dead, saw Jesus do good deeds, and watched Jesus cover people's shortcomings and transgressions, Peter could believe, 'He has indeed come from God.' In Matthew 16 we can find his confession.

"Who do you say that I am?" (v. 15)
"You are the Christ, the Son of the living God." (v. 16)

Then something unimaginable happened to Peter who could make such a bold confession as above. Peter even confessed to Jesus at the last supper, *"Even though all may fall away because of You, I will never fall away."* But the night Jesus was captured and crucified, Peter denied knowing Jesus three times in fear of death.

After Jesus resurrected and ascended into heaven, Peter received the Holy Spirit and was transformed in a marvelous way. He came to devote every ounce of his life to preaching the gospel of Jesus Christ without fearing death. One day 3,000 people repented and were baptized when he boldly testified to Jesus Christ. Even before the Jewish leaders who were threatening to take his life, he boldly proclaimed that Jesus Christ is our Lord and Savior.

"Repent, and each of you be baptized in the name of Jesus Christ for the forgiveness of your sins; and you will receive the gift of the Holy Spirit. For the promise is for you and your children and for all who

are far off, as many as the Lord our God will call to Himself" (Acts 2:38-39).

"He is the stone which was rejected by you, the builders, but which became the chief corner stone. And there is salvation in no one else; for there is no other name under heaven that has been given among men by which we must be saved" (Acts 4:11-12).

Peter displayed the power of God by manifesting many signs and wonders. At Lydda, Peter healed a man who had been paralyzed for eight years, and at the nearby Joppa, he revived Tabitha who had fallen sick and died. Peter also let the crippled stand up and walk, healed people suffering from a variety of diseases, and drove out demons.

God's power accompanied Peter to such an extent that people even carried the sick out into the streets and laid them on cots and pallets because they expected that when Peter came by at least his shadow might fall on any one of them (Acts 5:15).

In addition, God revealed to Peter through visions that the gospel of salvation was to be brought to the Gentiles. One day, when Peter went up on the housetop to pray, he felt hungry and desired to eat something. While food was being prepared, Peter fell into a trance and saw the sky opened up and an object like a great sheet coming down. There were in it all kinds of four-footed animals and crawling creatures of the earth and birds of the air (Acts 10:9-12). Peter then heard a voice.

"Get up, Peter, kill and eat!" (v. 13)
"By no means, Lord, for I have never eaten anything unholy and unclean." (v. 14)
"What God has cleansed, no longer consider unholy." (v. 15)

This happened three times, and everything was drawn back up into the sky. Peter could not understand why God commanded him to eat something defined "unclean" by Moses' Law. While Peter was pondering the vision, the Holy Spirit told him, *"Behold, three men are looking for you. But get up, go downstairs and accompany them without misgivings, for I have sent them Myself"* (Acts 10:19-20). The three men came on behalf of the Gentile Cornelius who sent for Peter to come to his house.

Through this vision, God revealed to Peter that God wanted His mercy to be preached even to the Gentiles, and urged Peter to spread the gospel of the Lord Jesus Christ to them. Peter was so grateful to the Lord who loved him to the end and entrusted him with a sacred task as His apostle even though he had denied Him three times that he did not spare his life in leading countless souls to the path to salvation, and died a martyr's death.

John the Apostle Prophesies on the Last Days by the Revelation of Jesus Christ

John was previously a fisherman in the Galilee, but after he was called on by Jesus, John always walked with Him and witnessed His manifestations of signs and wonders. John saw Jesus turning water into wine at the wedding in Cana, healing countless sick people including a person who had been sick for 38 years, driving out demons from many, and opening the eyes of the blind. John also witnessed Jesus walk on water and bring back to life Lazarus who had been dead for four days.

John followed Jesus when Jesus was transfigured (His face shone like the sun, and His garments became as white as light) and spoke with Moses and Elijah atop the Mount of Transfiguration. Even when Jesus was breathing His last on the cross, John heard Jesus speak to the Virgin Mary and him:

"Woman, behold, your son!"
"Behold, your mother!"

With this third last word that Jesus spoke on the cross, in physical terms Jesus was comforting Mary who had carried and given birth to Him but in spiritual sense He was proclaiming to all mankind that all believers were brothers, sisters, and mothers.

Jesus never referred to Mary as His "mother." As Jesus the Son of God is God Himself in essence, no one could have given birth to Him and He could not have a mother. The reason Jesus told John, "Behold, your mother!" was because John was to serve Mary as his mother. From that hour John took Mary into his own household and served her as his mother.

After Jesus' resurrection and ascension, he diligently preached the gospel of Jesus Christ along with other apostles despite the constant threats of the Jews. Through their fervent preaching of the gospel, the Early Church experienced spectacular revival, but at the same time the apostles were persistently subject to persecution.

John the Apostle was questioned in the Council of the Jews and later he was plunged into boiling oil by the Roman Emperor Domitian. But John suffered nothing from it by God's power and providence, and the Emperor exiled him to the Greek island of Patmos in the Mediterranean Sea. There, John communicated with God in prayer and by the inspiration of the Holy Spirit and the guidance of angels, he saw many deep visions and recorded the revelations of Jesus Christ.

> *The Revelation of Jesus Christ, which God gave Him to show to His bond-servants, the things which must soon take place; and He sent and communicated it by His angel to His bond-servant John (Revelation 1:1).*

In the inspiration of the Holy Spirit, John the Apostle wrote in detail of the things that would happen in the last days so that all people would accept Jesus as their Savior and prepare themselves to receive Him as the King of kings and the Lord of lords at His Second Coming.

Members of the Early Church Hold Fast to Their Faith

When the resurrected Jesus ascended into heaven, He promised His disciples that He would return in the same way they watched Him going into heaven.

The countless witnesses of Jesus' resurrection and ascension realized that they would also be able to resurrect and no longer came to fear death. That is how they could live their lives as His witnesses in the face of the threats and oppression of the rulers of the world and the persecution that often cost them their lives. Not only Jesus' disciples who had served Him during His public ministry but also countless others became prey to lions at the Colosseum in Rome, were beheaded, crucified, and burnt to ashes. However, all of them held fast to their faith in Jesus Christ.

As the persecution against Christians intensified, the members of the Early Church hid in Rome's catacombs, known as "underground burial places." Their lives were miserable; it was as though they were not really living. Because they had passionate and earnest love for the Lord, however, they did not fear any kind of trials and torment.

Before Christianity was officially recognized in Rome,

the oppression against Christians was harsh and cruel beyond description. Christians were stripped of their citizenship, the Bibles and churches were set ablaze, and church leaders and workers were arrested, brutally tortured, and executed.

Polycarp at the Smyrna church in Asia Minor had the personal fellowship with John the Apostle. Polycarp was a devoted bishop. When Polycarp was arrested by the Roman authorities and stood before the Governor, he did not forsake his faith.

"I do not want to disgrace you. Order those Christians to be killed and I will release you. Curse Christ!"

"For 86 years I have been His servant, and He has done me no wrong. How can I blaspheme my King who has saved me?"

They attempted to burn him to death, but because it failed, Polycarp the bishop of Smyrna died a martyr after being stabbed to death. When many other Christians witnessed and heard Polycarp's marches of faith and his martyrdom, they came to fathom the Passion of Jesus Christ all the more, and chose the path of martyrdom themselves.

Men of Israel, take care what you propose to do

with these men. For some time ago Theudas rose up, claiming to be somebody, and a group of about four hundred men joined up with him. But he was killed, and all who followed him were dispersed and came to nothing. After this man, Judas of Galilee rose up in the days of the census and drew away some people after him; he too perished, and all those who followed him were scattered. So in the present case, I say to you, stay away from these men and let them alone, for if this plan or action is of men, it will be overthrown; but if it is of God, you will not be able to overthrow them; or else you may even be found fighting against God (Acts 5:35-39).

As the renowned Gamaliel exhorted and reminded the people of Israel as above, the gospel of Jesus Christ who came from God Himself could not be toppled. Finally in 313 A.D., Emperor Constantine recognized Christianity as the official religion of his empire and the gospel of Jesus Christ began to be preached to the whole world.

The Testimony on Jesus Recorded in Pilate's Report

Among historical documents from the times of the Roman Empire, there is a manuscript on Jesus' resurrection which Pontius Pilate, Governor of the Roman Province of Judea during Jesus' time, wrote and sent to the Emperor.

51
Israel: God's Elect

The following is an excerpt on the event of the resurrection of Jesus from "Pilate's Report to Caesar of the Arrest, Trial, and Crucifixion of Jesus," currently kept in the Hagia Sophia in Istanbul, Turkey:

A few days after the sepulcher was found empty, his disciples proclaimed all over the country that Jesus had risen from the dead, as He had foretold. This created more excitement even than the crucifixion. As to its truth I cannot say for certain, but I have made some investigation of the matter; so you can examine for yourself, and see if I am in fault, as Herod represents.

Joseph buried Jesus in his own tomb. Whether he contemplated His resurrection or calculated to cut him another, I cannot tell. The day after he was buried one of the priests came to the praetorium and said they were apprehensive that his disciples intended to steal the body of Jesus and hide it, and then make it appear that he had risen from the dead, as He had foretold, and of which they were perfectly convinced.

I sent him to the captain of the royal guard (Malcus) to tell him to take the Jewish soldiers, place as many around the sepulcher as were needed; then if anything should happen they could blame themselves and not the Romans.

When the great excitement arose about the sepulcher being found empty, I felt a deeper solicitude than ever. I sent for this man Islam, who related to me as near as I can recollect the following circumstances. They saw a soft and beautiful light over the sepulcher. He, at first, thought that the women had come to embalm the body of Jesus, as was their custom, but he could not see how they had gotten through the guards. While these thoughts were passing through his mind, behold the whole place was lightened up and there seemed to be crowds of the dead in their grave clothes.

All seemed to be shouting and filled with ecstasy, while all around and above was the most beautiful music he had ever heard and the whole air seemed to be full of voices praising God. All this time there seemed to be a reeling and swimming of the earth that he seemed to sicken and faint and he could not stand on his feet. He said the earth seemed to swim from under him, and his senses left him, so he knew not just what did occur.

As we read in Matthew 27:51-53, *"The earth shook and the rocks were split. The tombs were opened, and many bodies of the saints who had fallen asleep were raised; and coming out of the tombs after His resurrection they entered the holy city and appeared to many,"* the Roman guards gave identical testimony.

After recording the testimonies of the Roman guards who had witnessed spiritual phenomena, Pilate remarked towards the end of his report, "I am almost ready to say: 'Truly this was the Son of God.'"

Countless Witnesses of the Lord Jesus Christ

Not only Jesus' disciples who had served Him during His public ministry did bear witness to the gospel of Jesus Christ. Just as Jesus said in John 14:13, *"Whatever you ask in My name, that will I do, so that the Father may be glorified in the Son,"* countless witnesses have received God's answers to their prayer and testified to the living God and the Lord Jesus Christ since His resurrection and ascension into heaven.

But you will receive power when the Holy Spirit has come upon you; and you shall be My witnesses both in Jerusalem, and in all Judea and Samaria, and even to the remotest part of the earth (Acts 1:8).

I accepted the Lord after being healed by God's power of all my diseases against which medical science had been utterly helpless. Later I was anointed to be a servant of the Lord Jesus Christ and have been preaching the gospel to all peoples and manifesting signs and wonders.

As promised in the above verse, many people have become God's children by receiving the Holy Spirit and dedicated their lives to preaching the gospel of Jesus Christ with the power of the Holy Spirit. That is how the gospel has been spread to the whole world and countless people today are meeting the living God and accepting Jesus Christ.

Go into all the world and preach the gospel to all creation. He who has believed and has been baptized shall be saved; but he who has disbelieved shall be condemned. These signs will accompany those who have believed: in My name they will cast out demons, they will speak with new tongues; they will pick up serpents, and if they drink any deadly poison, it will not hurt them; they will lay hands on the sick, and they will recover (Mark 16:15-18).

Church of the Holy Sepulchre at Golgotha, the Hill of Calvary, in Jerusalem

Chapter 2

THE MESSIAH SENT BY GOD

God Promises the Messiah

Israel had often lost the sovereignty and had to suffer from invasions and the rule of the likes of Persia and Rome. Through His prophets, God gave a great deal of promises about the Messiah who was to come as the King of Israel. There could have been no greater sources of hope for the afflicted Israelites than God's promises on the Messiah.

> *For a child will be born to us, a son will be given to us; And the government will rest on His shoulders; And His name will be called Wonderful Counselor, Mighty God, Eternal Father, Prince of Peace. There will be no end to the increase of His government or of peace, On the throne of David and over his kingdom, To establish it and to uphold it with justice and righteousness From then on and forevermore The zeal of the LORD of hosts will accomplish this (Isaiah 9:6-7).*

> *"Behold, the days are coming," declares the LORD, "When I will raise up for David a righteous Branch; And He will reign as king and act wisely And*

do justice and righteousness in the land. In His days Judah will be saved, And Israel will dwell securely; And this is His name by which He will be called, 'The LORD our righteousness'" (Jeremiah 23:5-6).

Rejoice greatly, O daughter of Zion! Shout in triumph, O daughter of Jerusalem! Behold, your king is coming to you; He is just and endowed with salvation, Humble, and mounted on a donkey, Even on a colt, the foal of a donkey. I will cut off the chariot from Ephraim And the horse from Jerusalem; And the bow of war will be cut off And He will speak peace to the nations; And His dominion will be from sea to sea, And from the River to the ends of the earth (Zechariah 9:9-10).

Israel has been waiting for the Messiah without ceasing to this day. What is delaying the coming of the Messiah whom Israel eagerly awaits and anticipates? Many Jews want an answer to this question but the answer is found in the fact that they do not know that the Messiah already came.

Jesus the Messiah Suffered Just as Prophesied by Isaiah

The Messiah whom God promised Israel and really sent is Jesus. Jesus was born in Bethlehem in Judea some two thousand years ago and when the hour came, Jesus died on the cross, resurrected, and opened to all mankind the path to salvation. The Jews of His time, however, did not acknowledge Jesus as the Messiah for whom they had been waiting. It was because Jesus looked totally different from the image of the Messiah whom they had anticipated.

The Jews became weary from extended periods of colonial rule, and expected a potent Messiah to deliver them from their political strife. They thought that the Messiah would come as the King of Israel, put an end to all wars, deliver them from persecution and oppression, give them true peace, and magnify them above all nations.

However, Jesus did not come into this world in splendor and majesty befitting royalty but was born as the son of a poor carpenter. He did not even come to set Israel free from Rome's oppression or to restore its former glory. He came into this world to restore mankind who were doomed to destruction since Adam's sin and to make them the children of God.

For these reasons, the Jews did not acknowledge Jesus as the Messiah and instead crucified Him. If we study the image of the Messiah as recorded in the Bible, however, we can only affirm the fact that the Messiah is indeed Jesus.

For He grew up before Him like a tender shoot,
And like a root out of parched ground; He has no
stately form or majesty That we should look upon

Him, Nor appearance that we should be attracted to Him. He was despised and forsaken of men, A man of sorrows and acquainted with grief; And like one from whom men hide their face He was despised, and we did not esteem Him (Isaiah 53:2-3).

God told the Israelites that the Messiah, King of Israel, would have no stately form or majesty or appearance to attract us but instead He would be despised and forsaken by men. Still, the Israelites failed to recognize Jesus as the Messiah whom God had promised them.

He was despised and forsaken by God's elect the Israelites, but God set Jesus Christ above all nations and countless people to this day have accepted Him as their Savior.

As written in Psalm 118:22-23, *"The stone which the builders rejected Has become the chief corner stone. This is the LORD's doing; It is marvelous in our eyes,"* the providence of the salvation of mankind has been achieved by Jesus whom Israel abandoned.

Jesus did not have the appearances of the Messiah whom the people of Israel had expected to see, but we can understand that Jesus is the Messiah about whom God prophesied through His prophets.

Everything including glory, peace, and restoration that God promised us through the Messiah pertains to the spiritual realm and Jesus who came into this world to fulfill the task of the Messiah said, *"My kingdom is not of this world"* (John 18:36).

The Messiah about whom God prophesied was not a king with earthly authorities and glory. The Messiah was not to come to this world so that God's children might enjoy the wealth, reputation, and honor during their temporary life in this world. He was to come to save His people from their sins and to lead them to enjoy eternal joy and glory in heaven for ever and ever.

> *Then in that day The nations will resort to the root of Jesse, Who will stand as a signal for the peoples; And His resting place will be glorious (Isaiah 11:10).*

The promised Messiah was not to come just for God's elect the Israelites but also to fulfill the promise of salvation for all who accept God's promise on the Messiah by faith following the footsteps of Abraham's faith. In short, the Messiah was to come to fulfill God's promise of salvation as the Savior of all the nations of the earth.

The Need for the Savior for All Mankind

Why was the Messiah to come into this world not only for the salvation of the people of Israel but also that of all mankind?

In Genesis 1:28, God blessed Adam and Eve and told them, *"Be fruitful and multiply, and fill the earth, and subdue it; and rule over the fish of the sea and over the birds of the sky and over every living thing that moves on the earth."*

After creating the first man Adam and establishing him as the master of all other creatures, God gave the man the authority to "subdue" and "rule over" the earth. But when Adam ate of the tree of the knowledge of good and evil, which God had specifically forbidden him, and committed the sin of disobedience at the temptation by the Satan-instigated serpent, Adam could no longer enjoy such authority.

When they obeyed the word of righteousness of God, Adam and Eve were slaves to righteousness and enjoyed the authorities that God had given them, but after they sinned, they since became slaves to sin and the devil, and were forced to relinquish the authorities (Romans 6:16). Thus, all the authority that Adam received from God was handed over to the devil.

In Luke 4, the enemy devil tempted Jesus, who had just finished fasting for 40 days, three times. The devil showed Jesus all the kingdoms of the world and said to Him, *"I will give You all this domain and its glory; for it has been handed over to me, and I give it to whomever I wish. Therefore if You worship before me, it shall all be Yours"* (Luke 4:6-7). The devil implies that the "domain and its glory" was "handed over to me" from Adam and the devil can also hand it over to someone else as well.

Yes, Adam lost all the authority and handed over it to the devil, and as a result he became a slave of the devil. Since then Adam added sin upon sin under the control of the devil, and was placed on the path to death, which is the wages of sin. This did not stop with Adam but affected all of his descendants, who were to inherit Adam's original sin through hereditary influences. They were also placed under the authority of sin governed by the devil and Satan and destined to death.

This accounts for the necessity of the coming of the Messiah. Not only God's elect the Israelites but also all peoples of the world needed the Messiah who would be able to deliver them from the authority of the devil and Satan.

Qualifications of the Messiah

Just as there are laws in this world, there are rules and regulations also in the spiritual realm. Whether a person will fall into death or receive forgiveness of his sins and arrive at salvation depends on the law of the spiritual realm.

What qualifications must a person satisfy in order to become the Messiah to save all mankind from the curses of the Law?

The provision concerning the qualifications of the Messiah is found in the law that God gave to His elect. The law was concerning the redemption of the land.

> *The land, moreover, shall not be sold permanently, for the land is Mine; for you are but aliens and sojourners with Me. Thus for every piece of your property, you are to provide for the redemption of the land. If a fellow countryman of yours becomes so poor he has to sell part of his property, then his nearest kinsman is to come and buy back what his relative has sold (Leviticus 25:23-25).*

The Law on the Redemption of the Land Contains Secrets on the Qualifications of the Messiah

God's elect the Israelites abided by the law. Thus, during a transaction to sell and buy land, they strictly adhered to the law on the redemption of the land recorded in the Bible. Unlike the land law in other countries, Israel's law made it clear in the contract that the land was not to be sold permanently but it could be purchased back at a later time. It provides that a wealthy kinsman can redeem the land for a member of his family who sold it. If the person has no kinsman enough wealthy to redeem it but he has recovered his means enough for its redemption, the law allows the original owner of the land to redeem it for himself.

How, then, is the law on the redemption of the land in Leviticus related to the qualifications of the Messiah?

In order to understand this better, we have to keep in mind the fact that man was formed of dust from the ground. In Genesis 3:19, God told Adam, *"By the sweat of your face You will eat bread, Till you return to the ground, Because from it you were taken; For you are dust, And to dust you shall return."* And it reads in Genesis 3:23, *"Therefore the LORD God sent him out from the garden of Eden, to cultivate the ground from which he was taken."*

God told Adam, "For you are dust," and "the land" spiritually signifies that man formed of dust from the ground.

So, the law on the redemption of the land concerning the selling and buying of land is directly related to the law of the spiritual realm concerning the salvation of mankind.

According to the law on the redemption of the land, God owns all the land and no man can permanently sell it. By the same token, all the authority that Adam received from God originally belonged to God and no one could thus sell it permanently. If one became poor and sold his land, the land was to be redeemed when an appropriate person appeared. Likewise, the devil had to return the authority handed over to it from Adam when an individual who could redeem that authority appeared.

Based on the law on the redemption of the land, the God of love and justice prepared an individual who could recover all the authority that Adam had handed over to the devil. That individual is the Messiah, and the Messiah is Jesus Christ who had been prepared from everlasting and was sent by God Himself.

Qualifications of the Savior and Their Fulfillment by Jesus Christ

Let us examine why Jesus is the Messiah and Savior of all mankind based on the law on the redemption of the land.

First, just as the redeemer of the land must be a kinsman, the Savior must also be a man to redeem mankind from their sins because all mankind became sinners through the sin of the first man Adam. Leviticus 25:25 tells us, *"If a fellow countryman of yours becomes so poor he has to sell part of his property, then his nearest kinsman is to come and buy back what his relative has sold."* If a person could no longer afford to retain his land and sold the land, his nearest kinsman could buy back the land. By the same token, because the first man Adam sinned and had to hand over to the devil the authority God had given him, the redemption of the authority handed over to the devil can and must be accomplished by a man, Adam's "nearest kinsman."

As we find in 1 Corinthians 15:21, *"For since by a man came death, by a man also came the resurrection of the dead,"* the Bible reaffirms to us that the redemption of sinners could be accomplished not by angels or beasts but only by man. Mankind was placed onto the path to death on account of the sin of Adam the first man, someone else had to redeem them from their sin, and only a fellow man, Adam's "nearest kinsman" could do it.

Although Jesus possessed the human nature as well as the divine nature as the Son of God, He was born of a human being in order to redeem mankind from their sins (John 1:14) and experienced growth. As a human being, Jesus slept and felt hunger and thirst, joy and sorrow. When He was hung on the cross, Jesus bled and felt the accompanying pain.

Even in the historical context, there is a piece of undeniable proof attesting to the fact that Jesus came into this world as a human being. With the birth of Jesus as a reference point, the history of the world is divided into two: "B.C." and "A.D." "B.C." or "Before Christ" refers to the era before Jesus' birth and "A.D." or "Anno Domini" ("In The year of Our Lord") refers to the time since the birth of Jesus. This fact affirms that Jesus came into this world as a man. Thus, Jesus satisfies the first qualification of the Savior because He came into this world as a man.

Second, just as the redeemer of the land could not redeem the land if he were poor, a descendant of Adam cannot redeem mankind from their sins because Adam sinned and all his descendants are born with original sin. The person for the Savior of all mankind must not be a descendant of Adam.

If a brother wanted to pay back the debt of his sister, he himself must be without any debt. In the same way, a person to redeem others from their sins must also be without sin. If the redeemer is sinful, he finds himself a slave to sin. How, then, can he possibly redeem others from their sins?

After Adam committed the sin of disobedience, all of his descendants have been born with the original sin. Thus, no descendant of Adam could ever be the Savior.

Fleshly speaking, Jesus is the descendant of David and His parents are Joseph and Mary. Matthew 1:20, however, tells us, *The Child who has been conceived in her is of the Holy*

Spirit."

The reason that every individual is born with the original sin is because he inherits his parents' sinful attributes through his father's sperm and his mother's egg. Yet, Jesus was not conceived from Joseph's sperm and Mary's egg but by the power of the Holy Spirit. It was because she became pregnant before they slept together. The almighty God can cause a child to be conceived by the power of the Holy Spirit without the union of a sperm and an egg.

Jesus merely "borrowed" the body of Mary the virgin. As He was conceived by the power of the Holy Spirit, Jesus did not inherit any attributes of the sinners. As Jesus is not a descendant of Adam and is without the original sin, He also satisfies the second qualification of the Savior.

Third, just as the redeemer of the land must be wealthy enough to redeem the land, the Savior of all mankind must have power to defeat the devil and save mankind from the devil.

Leviticus 25:26-27 tell us, *"Or in case a man has no kinsman, but so recovers his means as to find sufficient for its redemption, then he shall calculate the years since its sale and refund the balance to the man to whom he sold it, and so return to his property."* In other words, for a person to buy back the land, he has to possess "the means" to do so.

Rescuing the prisoners of war requires that one party should have the power to defeat the enemy and paying back the debt of others requires that the individual should have the financial means. By the same token, delivering all mankind from the authority of the devil requires that the Savior should possess the power to defeat the devil to rescue them from the devil.

Prior to his sinning, Adam possessed the power to rule over all creatures, but after his sinning, Adam became subject to the authority of the devil. From this we can infer that the power to defeat the devil comes from the sinlessness.

Jesus the Son of God was completely without sin. Because Jesus was conceived by the Holy Spirit and not a descendant of Adam, He was without the original sin. Furthermore, because He only abided by the Law of God throughout His life, Jesus had no sins which He committed. For this reason Peter the Apostle said that Jesus *"committed no sin, nor was any deceit found in His mouth; and while being reviled, He did not revile in return; while suffering, He uttered no threats, but kept entrusting Himself to Him who judges righteously"* (1 Peter 2:22-23).

As He was without any sin, Jesus had the power and authority to defeat the devil and had the power to save mankind from the devil. His countless manifestations of miraculous signs and wonders bear witness to this. Jesus healed sick people, drove out demons, made the blind see, the deaf hear, and the crippled walk. Jesus even calmed the violent sea and revived the dead.

The fact that Jesus was without sin was reaffirmed beyond any doubt by His resurrection. According to the law of the spiritual realm, sinners must face death (Romans 6:23). As He was without sin, however, Jesus was not placed under the power of death. He breathed His last on the cross and His body was buried into the tomb, but on the third day He resurrected.

Keep in mind that such great fathers of faith as Enoch and Elijah were lifted up into heaven alive without facing death because they were without sin and became wholly sanctified. Likewise, on the third day after He was buried, Jesus shattered the authority of the devil and Satan through His resurrection, and became the Savior of all mankind.

Fourth, just as the redeemer of the land must have love to redeem the land for his kinsman, the Savior of mankind must also possess love by which He could lay down His life for others.

Even if the Savior satisfies the first three qualifications mentioned earlier but does not have love, He could not become the Savior of all mankind. Suppose a brother has a debt of $100,000 and his sister is a multimillionaire. Without love, the sister would not pay back her brother's debt and her enormous wealth means nothing for the brother.

Jesus came into the world as a human being, was not a descendant of Adam, and had the power to defeat the devil and to save mankind from the devil because he had no sin at all. However, if He had lacked love, Jesus could not have redeemed mankind from their sins. "Jesus' redemption of mankind from their sins" means that He was to receive the punishment of death on their behalf. For Jesus to redeem mankind from their sins, He had to be crucified as one of the most heinous sinners in the world, to suffer all sorts of scorn and contempt, and to shed all His water and blood to death. Because Jesus' love for the mankind was so fervent and He was willing to redeem mankind from their sins, however, Jesus did not concern Himself with the punishment of the crucifixion.

Why, then, did Jesus have to be hung on a wooden cross and shed His blood to death? As Deuteronomy 21:23 tells us, *"He who is hanged [on the tree] is accursed of God,"* and according to the law of the spiritual realm dictating that "The wages of sin is death," Jesus was hung on the tree to redeem all mankind from the curse of sin to which they were bound.

Furthermore, as Leviticus 17:11 reads, *"For the life of the flesh is in the blood, and I have given it to you on the altar to make atonement for your souls; for it is the blood by reason of the life that makes atonement,"* there is no forgiveness of sins without the shedding of blood.

Of course, Leviticus tells us that fine flour could be offered to God instead of the blood of animals. This measure, however, was for those who were not able to afford to offer animals. It was not the kind of offering of blood with which God was pleased. Jesus redeemed us from our sins by being hung on the wooden cross and bleeding to death on it.

How marvelous Jesus' love is that Jesus shed His blood on the cross and opened the path to salvation for those who scorned and crucified Him, even though He healed people of all sorts of diseases, loosened the bonds of wickedness, and did only good?

Based on the law on the redemption of the land, we conclude that only Jesus satisfies the qualifications of the Savior who can redeem the mankind from their sins.

The Path to Salvation of Mankind Prepared Before the Ages

The path to salvation of mankind opened when Jesus died on the cross and resurrected on the third day of His burial shattering the authority of death. Jesus' coming into this world to fulfill the providence of the salvation of mankind and becoming the Messiah for mankind was predicted at the very moment when Adam sinned.

In Genesis 3:15, God told the serpent that tempted the woman, *"I will put enmity Between you and the woman, And between your seed and her seed; He shall bruise you on the head, And you shall bruise him on the heel."* Here, "the woman" spiritually symbolizes God's elect Israel and "the serpent" signifies the enemy devil and Satan which oppose God. When the seed of "the woman" would "bruise [the serpent] on the head," it means that the Savior of mankind would come among the Israelites and defeat the power of death of the enemy devil.

A serpent becomes powerless once its head is injured. In the same way, when God told the serpent that the seed of the woman would bruise the serpent on the head, He prophesied that the Christ for mankind would be born of Israel and destroy the authority of the devil and Satan and save sinners bound to their authority.

Because it became aware of this, the devil sought to kill the seed of the woman before He could inflict damage on its head. That is how the devil believed that it could forever enjoy the authority handed over from the disobedient Adam only if it would kill the seed of the woman. The enemy devil, however, did not know who the seed of the woman would be and thus began plotting to kill God's faithful and beloved prophets ever since Old Testament times.

When Moses was born, the enemy devil instigated Pharaoh of Egypt into killing all male children born of Israel's women (Exodus 1:15-22), and when Jesus came into this world in flesh, it moved the heart of King Herod and let him kill all the male children who were in Bethlehem and all its vicinity, from two years old and under. For that reason, God worked for Jesus' family and led them to escape to Egypt.

Afterwards Jesus grew under the care of God Himself, and began His ministry at the age of 30. According to God's will, Jesus went throughout all Galilee, teaching in their synagogues, and healing every kind of disease and every kind of sickness among the people, reviving the dead, and preaching the gospel of the kingdom of heaven to the poor.

The devil and Satan instigated the chief priests, the scribes, and the Pharisees, and began to plot ways to kill Jesus through them. But the evil ones could not even touch Jesus until the time of God's choosing. Only towards the end of Jesus' three-year ministry did God allow them to arrest and crucify Jesus to fulfill the providence of the salvation of mankind through Jesus' crucifixion.

Succumbing to the pressure from the Jews, Roman Governor Pontius Pilate sentenced Jesus to crucifixion, and thus Roman soldiers crowned Jesus with thorns and nailed through His hands and feet onto the cross.

Crucifixion was one of the cruelest methods to execute a criminal. When the devil succeeded in having Jesus crucified in that cruel way by evil men, how much the devil must have rejoiced! It expected that no one and nothing else would be able to hinder its reign over the world, and sang songs of joy with dancing. But God's providence was to be found here.

But we speak God's wisdom in a mystery, the hidden wisdom which God predestined before the ages to our glory; the wisdom which none of the rulers of this age has understood; for if they had understood it they would not have crucified the Lord of glory (1 Corinthians 2:7-8).

Because God is just, He does not exercise the absolute authority to the point of breaking the law but does everything in accordance with the law of the spiritual realm. Thus, He had paved the path to the salvation of mankind before the ages in accordance with the law of God.

According to the law of the spiritual realm, saying, "the wages of sin is death" (Romans 6:23), if an individual does not sin, he cannot arrive at death. However, the devil crucified the sinless, unblemished, and spotless Jesus. The devil therefore violated the law of the spiritual realm and had to pay the penalty by giving back the authority Adam had handed over to it after committing the sin of disobedience. In other words, the devil was now forced to relinquish their hold on all people who would accept Jesus as their Savior and believe in His name.

Had the enemy devil known this wisdom of God, it would not have crucified Jesus. Because it had no idea of this secret, however, it had the sinless Jesus killed, firmly believing that it would ensure its grip on the world for ever. But in reality the devil fell into its own snare, and ended up violating the law of the spiritual realm. How marvelous God's wisdom is!

The truth is that the enemy devil became the instrument in fulfilling God's providence of the salvation of mankind and as prophesied in Genesis its head was "bruised" by the seed of the woman.

By God's providence and wisdom, the sinless Jesus died in order to redeem all mankind from their sins, and by resurrecting on the third day, He shattered the authority of death of the enemy devil and became the King of kings and the Lord of lords. He opened the door to salvation so that we can become justified through the faith in Jesus Christ.

Therefore, countless people throughout the history of mankind have been saved through the faith in Jesus Christ and so many more today are accepting the Lord Jesus Christ.

Receiving the Holy Spirit through the Faith in Jesus Christ

Why do we receive salvation when we believe in Jesus Christ? Upon accepting Jesus Christ as our Savior, we receive the Holy Spirit from God. When we receive the Holy Spirit, our spirits, which have been dead, are revived. As the Holy Spirit is the power and the heart of God, the Holy Spirit leads God's children onto the truth and helps them live by God's will.

Thus, those who truly believe Jesus Christ to be their Savior will follow the desires of the Holy Spirit and strive to live by God's word. They will rid themselves of hatred, hot-temper, jealousy, envy, judging and condemning of others, and adultery, and instead walk in goodness and truth and understand, serve, and love others.

As mentioned earlier, when the first man Adam sinned by eating of the tree of the knowledge of good and evil, the spirit in man died and man was placed on the path to destruction.

But when we receive the Holy Spirit, our dead spirits are revived and as much as we seek the desires of the Holy Spirit and walk in the word of truth of God, we gradually become men of the truth and recover the lost image of God.

When we walk in the word of truth of God, our faith will be recognized as "true faith," and because our sins will be cleansed by the blood of Jesus according to our deeds of faith, we can receive salvation. For that reason, 1 John 1:7 tells us, *"If we walk in the Light as [God] Himself is in the Light, we have fellowship with one another, and the blood of Jesus His Son cleanses us from all sin."*

This is how we arrive at salvation by faith after receiving forgiveness of our sins. However, if we walk in sin despite our confession of faith, that confession is a lie, and thus, the blood of our Lord Jesus Christ cannot redeem us from our sins nor can He warrant us salvation.

Of course, it is a different story for people who have just received Jesus Christ. Even if they are not yet walking in the truth, God will examine their heart, believe that they will be transformed, and lead them to salvation when they strive to march towards the truth.

Jesus Fulfills the Prophecies

God's word on the Messiah prophesied through the prophets was fulfilled by Jesus. Every aspect of the life of Jesus, from His birth and ministry to His death and the crucifixion and resurrection, was within the providence of God for Him to become the Messiah and Savior for all mankind.

Jesus Born of a Virgin in Bethlehem

God prophesied the birth of Jesus through Prophet Isaiah. At the time of God's choosing, the power of God the Most High descended on a woman of purity named Mary in Nazareth in the Galilee and she soon became pregnant with a child.

Therefore the Lord Himself will give you a sign: Behold, a virgin will be with child and bear a son, and she will call His name Immanuel (Isaiah 7:14).

Just as God promised the people of Israel, *"There will be no end to the line of kings in the House of David,"* He caused the Messiah to come from a woman named Mary, who was due to be married to Joseph, a descendant of David. As a descendant of Adam born with the original sin could not redeem mankind from their sins, God fulfilled the prophecy by having Mary the virgin give birth to Jesus before she and Joseph married.

But as for you, Bethlehem Ephrathah, Too little to be among the clans of Judah, From you One will go forth for Me to be ruler in Israel His goings forth are from long ago, From the days of eternity (Micah 5:2).

The Bible prophesied that Jesus would be born in Bethlehem. Indeed, Jesus was born in Bethlehem in Judea during the time of King Herod (Matthew 2:1), and history attests to this event.

When Jesus was born, King Herod feared the threat on his rule, and tried to have Jesus killed. Because he was unable to find the baby, however, King Herod killed all the male children in Bethlehem and all its vicinity, from two years old and under and thus there were weeping and mourning throughout the region.

If Jesus had not come into this world as the true King of the Jews, why would a king have sacrificed so many children to kill one baby? This tragedy was made because the enemy devil that sought to kill the Messiah out of fear of losing the reign over the world moved the heart of King Herod who was afraid of the loss of his crown and let him commit that atrocity.

Jesus Testifies to the Living God

Prior to beginning His ministry, Jesus wholly kept the Law for the thirty years of His life. And when He became old enough to become a priest, He began carrying out His ministry to become the Messiah as planned before the ages.

The Spirit of the LORD God is upon me, Because the LORD has anointed me To bring good news to the afflicted; He has sent me to bind up the brokenhearted, To proclaim liberty to captives And freedom to prisoners; To proclaim the favorable year of the LORD And the day of vengeance of our God; To comfort all who mourn, To grant those who mourn in Zion, Giving them a garland instead of ashes, The oil of gladness instead of mourning, The mantle of praise instead of a spirit of fainting. So they will be called oaks of righteousness, The planting of the LORD, that He may be glorified. (Isaiah 61:1-3).

As we find in the prophecy above, Jesus resolved all problems of life with the power of God and comforted the brokenhearted. And when the time of God's choosing came, Jesus went into Jerusalem to suffer the Passion.

Rejoice greatly, O daughter of Zion! Shout in triumph, O daughter of Jerusalem! Behold, your king is coming to you; He is just and endowed with salvation, Humble, and mounted on a donkey, Even on a colt, the foal of a donkey (Zechariah 9:9).

According to Zechariah's prophecy, Jesus entered the city of Jerusalem riding on a colt. The crowds shouted, *"Hosanna to the Son of David; Blessed is He who comes in the name of the Lord; Hosanna in the highest!" (Matthew 21:9)*, and there was excitement throughout the city. The people rejoiced that way because Jesus manifested such wondrous signs and wonders as walking on water and reviving the dead. Soon, however, the crowds would betray and crucify Him.

When they saw how large crowds followed Jesus to hear His words of authority and to see manifestations of God's power, priests, the Pharisees, and the scribes felt their position in the society was threatened. Out of harsh hatred of this Jesus, they plotted to kill Him. They produced all sorts of false proof against Jesus and accused Him deceiving and inciting the people. Jesus displayed marvelous works of God's power that could not otherwise have been performed unless God Himself was with Him, but they tried to get rid of Jesus.

In the end, one of Jesus' disciples betrayed Him and the priests paid him thirty pieces of silver for helping them arrest Jesus. Zechariah's prophecies on thirty pieces of silver in wages, saying, *"I took the thirty shekels of silver and threw them to the potter,"* was fulfilled (Zechariah 11:12-13).

Later the man who betrayed Jesus for thirty pieces of silver, was unable to overcome the sense of guilt, and threw the thirty pieces of silver into the temple sanctuary, but the priests spent that money to purchase a "potter's land" (Matthew 27:3-10).

The Passion and the Death of Jesus

As Prophet Isaiah prophesied, Jesus suffered the Passion in order to save all people. Because Jesus came into this world to fulfill the providence of redeeming His people from their sins, He was hung and died on the wooden cross that was the symbol of the curse and was sacrificed to God as a guilt offering for mankind.

Surely our griefs He Himself bore, And our sorrows He carried; Yet we ourselves esteemed Him stricken, Smitten of God, and afflicted. But He was pierced through for our transgressions, He was crushed for our iniquities; The chastening for our well-being fell upon Him, And by His scourging we are healed. All of us like sheep have gone astray, Each of us has turned to his own way; But the LORD has caused the iniquity of us all To fall on Him. He was oppressed and He was afflicted, Yet He did not open His mouth; Like a lamb that is led to slaughter, And like a sheep that is silent before its shearers, So He did not open His mouth. By oppression and judgment He was taken away; And as for His generation, who considered

That He was cut off out of the land of the living For the transgression of my people, to whom the stroke was due? His grave was assigned with wicked men, Yet He was with a rich man in His death, Because He had done no violence, Nor was there any deceit in His mouth. But the LORD was pleased To crush Him, putting Him to grief; If He would render Himself as a guilt offering, He will see His offspring, He will prolong His days, And the good pleasure of the LORD will prosper in His hand (Isaiah 53:4-10).

During Old Testament times, blood of animals was offered to God each time an individual sinned against Him. But Jesus shed His pure blood that included neither original sin nor self-committed sin and "offered one sacrifice for sins for all time" so that all men might receive the forgiveness of their sins and go to eternal life (Hebrews 10:11-12). Thus, He paved the way for the forgiveness of sins and the salvation through the faith in Jesus Christ and we no longer need to sacrifice the blood of animals.

When Jesus breathed His last on the cross, the veil of the temple was torn in two from top to bottom (Matthew 27:51). The veil of the temple was a large curtain separating the Holy of Holies from the Holy Place in the Temple, and no ordinary people could enter the Holy Place. Only the high priest could enter the Holy of Holies once a year.

The fact that "the veil of the temple was torn in two from

top to bottom" symbolizes that when He sacrificed Himself as the propitiation Jesus destroyed the wall of sin standing between God and us. In Old Testament times, high priests had to offer sacrifices to God for the redemption of the people of Israel from their sins and prayed to God on their behalf. Now that the wall of sin standing on our way to God was destroyed, we can communicate with God ourselves. In other words, anyone who believes in Jesus Christ can enter the holy sanctuary of God and worship Him and pray to Him there.

I will allot Him a portion with the great, And He will divide the booty with the strong; Because He poured out Himself to death, And was numbered with the transgressors; Yet He Himself bore the sin of many, And interceded for the transgressors (Isaiah 53:12).

Just as Prophet Isaiah recorded on the Passion and Crucifixion of the Messiah, Jesus died on the cross for the sins of all people but was numbered with the transgressors. Even while He was dying on the cross, He asked God to forgive those who were crucifying Him.

Father, forgive them; for they do not know what they are doing (Luke 23:34).

When He died on the cross, the Psalmist's prophecy, *"He keeps all his bones, Not one of them is broken"* (Psalm 34:20) was fulfilled. We can find its fulfillment in John 19:32-33, *"So the soldiers came, and broke the legs of the first man and of the other who was crucified with Him; but coming to Jesus, when they saw that He was already dead, they did not break His legs."*

Jesus Fulfils His Ministry for Becoming the Messiah

Jesus bore the sins of mankind on His cross and died for them as the sin offering, but the fulfillment of the providence of salvation was not through Jesus' death.

As prophesied in Psalm 16:10, *"For You will not abandon my soul to Sheol; Nor will You allow Your Holy One to undergo decay,"* and in Psalm 118:17, *"I will not die, but live, And tell of the works of the LORD,"* Jesus' body was not decayed and He resurrected on the third day.

As further prophesied in Psalm 68:18, *"You have ascended on high, You have led captive Your captives; You have received gifts among men, Even among the rebellious also, that the LORD God may dwell there,"* Jesus ascended into heaven and has been waiting for the last days at which He will complete the cultivation of mankind and lead His people into heaven.

It is easily noted how everything that God prophesied on the Messiah through His prophets have been wholly accomplished through Jesus Christ.

Death of Jesus and Prophecies on Israel

God's elect Israel failed to recognize Jesus as the Messiah. Still, God has not forsaken the people He has chosen and is accomplishing today His providence of salvation of Israel.

Even through Jesus' crucifixion, God prophesied the future of Israel, and this is because of His earnest love for them and desire for them to believe in the Messiah whom God sent and to reach salvation.

The Suffering for Israel that Crucified Jesus

Even though Roman Governor Pontius Pilate sentenced Jesus to crucifixion, it was the Jews who persuaded Pilate to make that decision. Pilate was aware that there was no ground on which to kill Jesus, but the crowds pressured him, shouting for Jesus' crucifixion, to the extent of starting a riot.

Firming up his decision to crucify Jesus, Pilate took water and washed his hands in front of the crowd and said to them, *"I am innocent of this Man's blood; see to that yourselves"* (Matthew 27:24). In response, the Jews shouted, *"His blood shall be on us and on our children!"* (Matthew 27:25)

In 70 A.D., Jerusalem fell to Roman General Titus. The

Temple was destroyed and the survivors were forced to leave their homeland and scatter to the world. Thus the Diaspora began and it lasted nearly 2,000 years. During this period of the Diaspora the extent of the torment that the people of Israel endured cannot be adequately described with words.

When Jerusalem fell, about 1.1 million Jews were slaughtered, and during World War II, approximately six million Jews were massacred by the Nazis. When they were slaughtered by the Nazis, the Jews were stripped naked and this is reminiscent of the time when Jesus was crucified naked.

Of course, from Israel's perspective, they can argue that their suffering is not the result of having crucified Jesus. Looking back at the history of Israel, however, it can be easily noted that Israel and its people were protected by God and thrived when they lived by the will of God. When they distanced themselves from God's will, the Israelites were disciplined and subject to suffering and trials.

So we know that Israel's suffering was not without cause. If crucifying Jesus had been proper in God's sight, why would God have left Israel in the midst of unceasing and harsh affliction for a long time?

Jesus' Outer Garments and His Tunic, and the Future of Israel

Another incident that foreshadowed the things to befall Israel took place at the site of Jesus' crucifixion. As we read in Psalm

22:18, *"They divide my garments among them, And for my clothing they cast lots,"* the Roman soldiers took Jesus' outer garments and made four parts, a part to every soldier, while they cast lots for His tunic and one of the soldiers took it with him.

How is this event related to the future of Israel? As Jesus is the King of the Jews, Jesus' outer garments spiritually symbolize God's elect, the state of Israel and its people. When Jesus' outer garments were split into four parts and the shape of the garments disappeared, this foreshadowed the destruction of the state of Israel. However, because the fabric of the outer garments remained, the event also foretold that even while the state of Israel might disappear, the name "Israel" would remain.

What is the significance of the fact that the Roman soldiers took Jesus' outer garments and made four parts, a part to every soldier? This signifies that the people of Israel would be destroyed by Rome and would be scattered. This prophecy was also fulfilled with the fall of Jerusalem and the destruction of the state of Israel, which forced the Jews to scatter to different parts of the world.

Of Jesus' tunic, John 19:23 reads, *"Now the tunic was seamless, woven in one piece."* The fact that His tunic was "seamless" signifies that no multiple layers of cloth were sewn together to form this piece of clothing.

Most people do not give much thought to how their clothes were woven. Why, then, does the Bible record in detail the structure of Jesus' tunic? In this is a prophecy of events to take place for the people of Israel.

Jesus' tunic symbolizes the heart of the people of Israel, the heart with which they serve God. The fact that the tunic was "seamless, woven in one piece" signifies Israel's heart towards God has lasted from their forefather Jacob and does not waver in any circumstances.

Through the Twelve Tribes following the times of Abraham, Isaac, and Jacob, they formed a nation and the people of Israel have held fast to their purity as a nation without intermarrying with the Gentiles. After the split into the Kingdom of Israel in the north and the Kingdom of Judah in the south, people in the northern kingdom intermarried but Judah remained a homogenous nation. Even today, the Jews maintain their identity that dates back to the times of fathers of faith.

Therefore, even though Jesus' outer garments were torn into four pieces, His tunic remained intact. This signifies that while the appearance of the state of Israel may disappear, the heart of the people Israel towards God and their faith in Him cannot be extinguished.

Because they have this unwavering heart, God chose them as His elect and through them He has been accomplishing His plan and will to this day. Even after the passing of millennia, the people of Israel are strictly adhering to the Law. This is because they have inherited Jacob's unchanging heart.

As a result, almost 1,900 years after they lost their country, the people of Israel shocked the world by declaring their independence and restoration of their statehood on May 14, 1948.

For I will take you from the nations, gather you from all the lands and bring you into your own land (Ezekiel 36:24).

You will live in the land that I gave to your forefathers; so you will be My people, and I will be your God (Ezekiel 36:28).

As already prophesied in the Old Testament, *"After many days you will be summoned; in the latter years,"* the people of Israel began flocking to Palestine and established a state again (Ezekiel 38:8). Moreover, by developing into one of the world's powerful countries, Israel has once again affirmed to the rest of the world their superior traits as a nation.

God Desires Israel to Prepare for Jesus' Return

God desires the newly-restored Israel to anticipate and prepare for the Return of the Messiah. Jesus came to the land of Israel approximately 2,000 years ago, completely fulfilled the providence of salvation for mankind and became the Savior and Messiah for them. When He ascended into heaven, He promised to return and now God wants His elect to wait for the return of the Messiah with true faith.

When the Messiah Jesus Christ comes again, He will not come in a shabby stable or have to suffer the punishment of the cross the way He did two millennia ago. Instead, He will appear in command of heavenly host and angels and return to this world as the King of kings and the Lord of lords in the glory of God for the whole world to see.

Behold, He is coming with the clouds, and every eye will see Him, even those who pierced Him; and all the tribes of the earth will mourn over Him. So it is to be (Revelation 1:7).

When the destined time comes, all people, believers and nonbelievers alike, will see the Lord's return in the air. On that day, all those who believe Jesus as the Savior of all mankind will be lifted up into the clouds and partake in the Wedding Banquet in the air, but the others will be left behind to mourn.

As God created the first man Adam and began the cultivation of mankind, there will surely be an end to it. Just as a farmer sows seeds and reaps the harvest, there will be a time of harvest for the cultivation of mankind as well. God's cultivation of mankind will be completed with the Second Advent of the Messiah Jesus Christ.

Jesus tells us in Revelation 22:7, *"And behold, I am coming quickly. Blessed is he who heeds the words of the prophecy of this book."* Our time is the last days. In His immeasurable love for Israel, God keeps enlightening His people through their history so that they will accept the Messiah. God earnestly desires not only His elect Israel but also all mankind to receive Jesus Christ before the end of the cultivation of mankind.

The Hebrew Bible, known to Christians as the Old Testament

Chapter **3**

THE GOD IN WHOM ISRAEL BELIEVES

The Law and the Tradition

While God was leading His chosen people, Israel, out of Egypt and into the promised land of Canaan, He descended unto the peak of Mt. Sinai. Then Jehovah called Moses, the leader of the Exodus, to Him and told him that the priests, who approached God, should consecrate themselves. In addition, God gave the people the Ten Commandments and many other laws through Moses.

When Moses had officially recounted all the words of Jehovah-God and the ordinances to the people, they answered with one voice and said, *"All the words which the LORD has spoken we will do!"* (Exodus 24:3) But while Moses was on the Mt. Sinai in accordance with the calling of God, the people had Aaron form the image of a calf and committed the great sin of worshipping the idol.

How is it that they could be God's chosen people and commit such a great sin? All men since Adam, who committed the sin of disobedience, are descendants of Adam and all have been born with sinful natures. They are compelled to sin before they have become sanctified through the circumcising of the heart. That is why God sent His only Son Jesus, and through Jesus' crucifixion He opened the gate to which mankind can be forgiven of all their sins.

Why then did God give the people the law? The Ten Commandments that God gave them through Moses, the ordinances and the decrees are known as the law.

Through the Law God Leads them into the Land Flowing with Milk and Honey

The reason and purpose that God gave the people of Israel the law on the Exodus from Egypt is for them to enjoy the blessing by which they could enter the land of Canaan, the land flowing with milk and honey. The people received the law directly from Moses, but they didn't keep the covenants of God and committed many sins including idol-worshiping and adultery. At last most of them died in their sins during 40 years of life in the desert.

The Book of Deuteronomy was recorded according to the last words of Moses, and delves into the covenants of God and the laws. When most of the first generation of Exodus but Joshua and Caleb died and the time of his leaving the people of Israel came, Moses eagerly urged the second and third generation of Exodus to love God and obey His commands.

Now, Israel, what does the Lord your God require from you, but to fear the LORD your God, to walk in all His ways and love Him, and to serve the LORD your God with all your heart and with all your soul, and to keep the LORD's commandments and His statutes which I am commanding you today for your good? (Deuteronomy 10:12-13).

God gave them the law because He wanted them to willingly obey it from the heart and to confirm their love for God through their obedience. God did not give them the law to restrict or bind them at all, but He wanted to accept their hearts of obedience and to give them blessings.

These words, which I am commanding you today, shall be on your heart. You shall teach them diligently to your sons and shall talk of them when you sit in your house and when you walk by the way and when you lie down and when you rise up. You shall bind them as a sign on your hand and they shall be as frontals on your forehead. You shall write them on the doorposts of your house and on your gates (Deuteronomy 6:6-9).

Through these verses, God told them how to bear the law in their hearts, teach it and practice it. Through the ages, the commands and ordinances of God as written in the Five

Books of Moses are still memorized and kept, but the focus on observing the law is outwardly expressed.

The Law and the Tradition of Elders

For example, the law commanded that the Sabbath be kept holy, and the elders regulated many detailed traditions that could evolve to observe the commandment such as prohibiting them from using the automatic doors, elevators and escalators and from opening business letters, passports, and other parcels. How did the traditions of elders come about?

When the Temple of God was destroyed and the people of Israel were taken away into the Babylonian Captivity, they thought it was because they had failed to serve God with all their hearts. They needed to serve God more properly and to apply the law to the situations that would change with the passing of time, so they made many strict regulations.

These regulations were established with a view to serving God wholeheartedly. In other words, they set up many strict regulations that detailed every aspect of life so that they could keep the law in their daily lives.

Sometimes the strict regulations played the role of protecting the law. But, as time went by they missed the true meaning embedded in the law and attached greater importance on the outward expression of observing the law. In this way they came to deviate from the true meaning of the law.

God sees and accepts the heart of each one in keeping the law rather than placing the importance on outward expression of observation of the law by deeds. So, He has set up the law in order to search for those who really honor Him, and to give blessing to those who obey Him. Though many people of Old Testament times seemed to keep the law, at the same time there were many who broke the law.

"Oh that there were one among you who would shut the gates, that you might not uselessly kindle fire on My altar! I am not pleased with you," says the LORD of hosts, "nor will I accept an offering from you" (Malachi 1:10).

When the teachers of the law and elders slandered against Jesus and condemned His disciples, it was not because Jesus and His disciples disobeyed the law, but because they violated the tradition of the elders. It is well described in the Gospel of Matthew.

Why do Your disciples break the tradition of the elders? For they do not wash their hands when they eat bread (Matthew 15: 2)

At this time, Jesus enlightened them to the fact that it was not the commandments of God that were broken, but instead, it was the traditions of elders that were broken. Of course, it is important to observe the law in action outwardly, but it is far more important to realize the true will of God that is embedded in the law.

And Jesus answered and said to them,

Why do you yourselves transgress the commandment of God for the sake of your tradition? For God said, 'Honor your father and mother,' and, 'He who speaks evil of father or mother is to be put to death.' But you say, 'Whoever says to his father or mother, "Whatever I have that would help you has been given to God," he is not to honor his father or his mother.' And by this you invalidated the word of God for the sake of your tradition (Matthew 15:3-6).

On the following verses, Jesus also says,

You hypocrites, rightly did Isaiah prophesy of you: 'This people honors Me with their lips, But their heart is far away from Me. But in vain do they worship Me, Teaching as doctrines the precepts of men' (Matthew 15:7-9).

After Jesus called the crowd to Him, He said to them,

Hear and understand. It is not what enters into the mouth that defiles the man, but what proceeds out of the mouth, this defiles the man (Matthew 15:10-11).

The children of God should honor their parents as written in the Ten Commandments. But the Pharisees taught the people that the children who are to serve and honor their parents with their possessions can be exempt from the duty if they pronounce that their possessions will be offered up to God. They made so many regulations detailing every aspect of life in such minute detail that the Gentiles could not even dare to strictly keep the traditions of the elders. They thought that they were doing very well as God's elect.

The God Israel Believes In

When Jesus healed the sick on the Sabbath day, the Pharisees condemned Jesus for breaking the Sabbath. One day Jesus entered into a synagogue and watched a man standing before the Pharisees there whose hand was withered. Jesus intended to awaken them and questioned them, saying the following:

Is it lawful to do good or to do harm on the Sabbath, to save a life or to kill? (Mark 3:4)

What man is there among you who has a sheep, and if it falls into a pit on the Sabbath, will he not take hold of it and lift it out? How much more valuable then is a man than a sheep! So then, it is lawful to do good on the Sabbath (Matthew 12:11-12).

Because the Pharisees had previously been filled with the frameworks of the law formed within the tradition of elders and the self-centered thoughts and manners of life, they not only failed to realize true will of God embedded in the law, but they also failed to recognize Jesus, who came down to the earth as the Savior.

Jesus often pointed out to them and urged them to repent and turn from their wrongdoings. He reproached them because they had neglected the true purpose of God for the law that He had given them, and changed and stuck to outward deeds of observing the law.

Woe to you, scribes and Pharisees, hypocrites! For you tithe mint and dill and cummin, and have neglected the weightier provisions of the law: justice and mercy and faithfulness; but these are the things you should have done without neglecting the others (Matthew 23:23).

Woe to you, scribes and Pharisees, hypocrites! For

you clean the outside of the cup and of the dish, but inside they are full of robbery and self-indulgence (Matthew 23:25).

The people of Israel, who were under the control of the Roman Empire, pictured in their mind that the Messiah would come for them with great power and honor and the Messiah would be able to set them free from the hands of the oppressors and rule over all the races of all nations.

Meanwhile a man was born of a carpenter; he kept company with the abandoned, the sick, and the sinners; he called God "Father," and he testified that *He is the Light of the world*. When he rebuked them for their sins, those who had kept the law by their own standard and declared themselves to be righteous, were pierced in their hearts and cut by his words and they crucified him without reason.

God Wants Us to Have Love and Forgiveness

The Pharisees have strictly observed the regulations of Judaism and counted long years of customs and traditions as valuable as their lives. They treated tax collectors, who worked for the Roman Empire, like sinners and avoided them.

Beginning in Matthew 9:10 it says that Jesus was reclining at the table in the house of a tax collector named Matthew, and many tax collectors and sinners were dining with Jesus and His disciples. When the Pharisees saw this, they said to His disciples, "Why is your Teacher eating with the tax collectors and sinners?" When Jesus heard them condemning His disciples, He explained to them about the heart of God. God gives His unfailing love and mercy to anyone who repents of his sins from the heart and turns from them.

Matthew 9:12-13 continues, *"But when Jesus heard this He said, 'It is not those who are healthy who need a physician, but those who are sick. But go and learn what this means: "I desire compassion, and not sacrifice," for I did not come to call the righteous, but sinners.'"*

When the wickedness of the people of Nineveh reached heaven, God was about to destroy the city of Nineveh. But, prior to doing so, God sent His prophet, Jonah, to let them repent of their sins. The people fasted and thoroughly repented of their sins, and God gave up His decision to destroy them. However, it was the Pharisees who thought that for anyone who breaks the law there is no other choice but to be judged. The most important part of the law is unfailing love and forgiveness, but the Pharisees thought that judging someone is more right and valuable than to forgive him with love.

In the same way, when we do not understand the heart of God who has given us the law, we are forced to judge everything with our own thoughts and theories and those judgments will be found wrong and against God.

God's True Purpose for Giving the Law

God created the heavens and the earth and everything in them and made man for the purpose of gaining true children who have resembled His heart. With this purpose God has told His people to *"be holy, for I am holy"* (Leviticus 11:44). He deems us to fear Him when we are not godly only in appearances but become blameless by throwing away evils from the heart.

In Jesus' time the Pharisees and scribes had much greater interest in offerings and in the actions of observing the law than in sanctifying their hearts. God delights in a broken and contrite heart rather than sacrifice (Psalm 51:16-17), so He has given us the law to let us repent of our sins and turn from them through the law.

God's True Will Embedded in the Law of the Old Testament

It does not follow that the people of Israel's actions of observing the law did not include their love for God at all. But the very thing that God wanted them to do is the sanctification of heart. That is why He seriously rebuked them through Prophet Isaiah.

"What are your multiplied sacrifices to Me?" Says the LORD. "I have had enough of burnt offerings of rams And the fat of fed cattle; And I take no pleasure in the blood of bulls, lambs or goats. When you come to appear before Me, Who requires of you this trampling of My courts? Bring your worthless offerings no longer, Incense is an abomination to Me. New moon and sabbath, the calling of assemblies I cannot endure iniquity and the solemn assembly" (Isaiah 1:11-13).

The true meaning of observing the law does not consist in outward actions but in the willingness of inner heart. So, God did not delight in the multiplied sacrifices that were offered only with habitual and superficial action of the entering into the holy courts. No matter how many sacrifices they offered according to the law, God took no delight in them because their hearts were not in accordance with the will of God.

It is the same with our prayers. In our prayers only the action of prayer is not important but the attitude of our hearts in prayers is much more important. A psalmist says in Psalm 66:18, *"If I regard wickedness in my heart, The LORD will not hear."*

God let the people know through Jesus that He does not delight in the prayers that are hypocritical or show off, but only sincere prayers from the heart.

When you pray, you are not to be like the hypocrites; for they love to stand and pray in the synagogues and on the street corners so that they may be seen by men. Truly I say to you, they have their reward in full. But you, when you pray, go into your inner room, close your door and pray to your Father who is in secret, and your Father who sees what is done in secret will reward you (Matthew 6:5-6).

The same happens when we repent of our sins. When we repent of our sins, God wants us not to tear our clothes and lament with ashes but to rend our hearts and repent of our sins from the heart. The action of the repentance itself is not important, and when we repent of our sins from the heart and turn from them, God accepts that repentance.

"Yet even now," declares the LORD, "Return to Me with all your heart, And with fasting, weeping and mourning; And rend your heart and not your garments. Now return to the LORD your God, For He is gracious and compassionate, Slow to anger, abounding in lovingkindness And relenting of evil" (Joel 2:12-13).

In other words, God wants to accept the heart of the doers of the law rather than the action of observing the law itself. This is described as the "circumcision of heart" in the Bible.

We can circumcise our bodies by cutting off the flesh of foreskin, while we can be circumcised in the skin of the heart through the cutting of our hearts.

The Circumcision of Heart that God Wants

To what does the circumcision of heart refer in detail? It refers to "cutting off and throwing away all kinds of evils and sins including envy, jealousy, hot-temper, ill feelings, adultery, falsehood, deceit, judging, and condemnation from the heart." When you cut off sins and evils from the heart and observe the law, God accepts it as perfect obedience.

Circumcise yourselves to the LORD and remove the foreskins of your heart, men of Judah and inhabitants of Jerusalem, or else My wrath will go forth like fire and burn with none to quench it, because of the evil of your deeds (Jeremiah 4:4).

So circumcise your heart, and stiffen your neck no longer (Deuteronomy 10:16).

Egypt and Judah, and Edom and the sons of Ammon, and Moab and all those inhabiting the desert who clip the hair on their temples; for all the nations are uncircumcised, and all the house of Israel are uncircumcised of heart (Jeremiah 9:26).

Moreover the LORD your God will circumcise your heart and the heart of your descendants, to love the LORD your God with all your heart and with all your soul, so that you may live (Deuteronomy 30:6).

Thus, the Old Testament often urges us to circumcise our hearts, for only those who are circumcised in their hearts can love God with all their hearts and all their souls.

God wants His children to be holy and perfect. In Genesis 17:1, God told Abraham to "be blameless," and in Leviticus 19:2, He commanded the people of Israel to "be holy."

John 10:35 says, *"If he called them gods, to whom the word of God came (and the Scripture cannot be broken),"* and 2 Peter 1:4 says, *"For by these He has granted to us His precious and magnificent promises, so that by them you may become partakers of the divine nature, having escaped the corruption that is in the world by lust."*

In Old Testament times they were saved through the actions of observing the law that was the symbol and shadow of the Messiah who was yet to come, while in New Testament times we can be saved through the faith in Jesus Christ who fulfilled the law with love.

Salvation through the actions, in Old Testament times, was possible when they had sinful desires to murder, hate, commit adultery, and lie, but did not commit them in actions. In Old

Testament times the Holy Spirit did not dwell in them and thus they could not cast off sinful desires with their own strength, so when they did not commit sins in actions outwardly, they were not considered as sinners.

However, in New Testament times, we can reach salvation only when we circumcise our hearts by faith. The Holy Spirit lets us know about sin, righteousness, and judgment and helps us live by the word of God, so we can cast off untruths and sinful natures and circumcise our hearts with the help of the Holy Spirit.

Salvation through the faith in Jesus Christ is not simply given when one knows and believes that Jesus Christ is the Savior. Only when we throw away evils from the heart because we love God and walk in the truth by faith, will God deem it to be true faith and guide us not only to complete salvation, but also to the path to amazing answers and blessing.

How to Please God

It is natural that a child of God should not sin in actions. It is also normal for him to cast off the untruths and sinful desires of the heart and to resemble the holiness of God. If you don't commit sins in actions but harbor sinful desires within you that God does not want, you cannot be deemed righteous by God.

That's why it is written in Matthew 5:27-28, *"You have heard that it was said, 'You shall not commit adultery'; but I say to you that everyone who looks at a woman with lust for her has already committed adultery with her in his heart."*

And it is said in 1 John 3:15, *"Everyone who hates his brother is a murderer; and you know that no murderer has eternal life abiding in him."* This verse urges us to get rid of hatred from the heart.

How do you have to act toward your enemies who hate you in accordance with the pleasing will of God?

The law of Old Testament times tells us, "Eye for eye [and] tooth for tooth." In other words, the law says, *"Just as he has injured a man, so it shall be inflicted on him."* It was to prevent one from injuring or causing harms to the other with strict regulations. It is because God knows that mankind tries to pay back the other with more than inflicted on him in his wickedness.

King David was commended as a person who was after the heart of God. When King Saul tried to kill him, David did not return any evil for the many evils of King Saul, but treated him with goodness to the last moment. David saw the true meaning embedded in the law and lived only by the word of God.

You shall not take vengeance, nor bear any grudge against the sons of your people, but you shall love your neighbor as yourself; I am the LORD (Leviticus 19:18).

Do not rejoice when your enemy falls, and do not let your heart be glad when he stumbles (Proverbs 24:17).

If your enemy is hungry, give him food to eat; and if he is thirsty, give him water to drink (Proverbs 25:21).

You have heard that it was said, 'You shall love your neighbor and hate your enemy.' But I say to you, love your enemies and pray for those who persecute you (Matthew 5:43-44).

According to the above verses, if you seem to observe the law but do not forgive a person who causes you troubles, God is not pleased with you. It is because God has told us to love our enemies. When you observe the law and when you do it with the heart God wants you to possess, you can be deemed to completely obey the word of God.

The Law, a Sign of God's Love

The God of love wants to give us endless blessings, but because He is the God of justice, He has no choice but to give out us to the devil as much as we commit sins. That's why some believers in God suffer from diseases and meet with accidents and disasters when they do not live by the word of God.

God has given us many commands in His love to protect us from those trials and pains. How many instructions do the parents give their children to protect them from diseases and accidents?

"Wash your hands when you come back home."
"Brush your teeth after eating."
"Look around when you cross the street."

In the same way, God has told us to observe His commandments and statutes for our good in His love (Deuteronomy 10:13). Keeping and practicing the word of God is like a lamp to our journey of life. No matter how dark it is, we can safely walk the path to destination with a lamp, and by the same token, when God who is light is with us, we can be protected and enjoy the privilege and blessing of the children of God.

How pleased God is when He protects His children who obey His word with His blazing eyes and gives them whatever they ask for! Accordingly those children can change their hearts into clean and good ones and resemble God as much as they keep and obey the word of God, and feel depths of God's love and they can love Him even more.

Therefore, the law that God has given us is like the textbook of love that presents the guideline to the best blessings for us who are under the cultivation of God on the earth. The law of God does not bring burdens on us but protects us from all kinds of disasters in this world which the enemy devil and Satan rule over and it guides us to the path of blessing.

Jesus Fulfilled the Law with Love

In Deuteronomy 19:19-21 we can find that in the times of the Old Testament when the people committed sins with their eyes, their eyes had to be plucked out. When they sinned with their hands or feet, then their hands or feet were cut off. When they murdered and committed adultery, they were stoned to death.

The law of the spiritual realm tells us that the result of our sins is death. That's why God seriously punished those who committed unforgivable sins, and thus He wanted to warn many other people not to commit the same sins.

But the God of love was not fully pleased with the faith by which they stuck to the law and said, "Eyes for eyes, and teeth for teeth." Instead He emphasized again and again in the Old Testament that they should circumcise their hearts. He did not want His people to feel pains due to the law, so when the time came, He sent Jesus to the earth and let Him take all the sins of mankind and fulfill the law with love.

Without Jesus' crucifixion, we would have our hands and feet cut off when we commit sins with our hands and feet. But Jesus took the cross and shed His precious blood by having His hands and feet nailed through to wash away all our sins that we committed with our hands and feet. Now we don't have to cut off our hands and feet because of this great love of God.

Jesus, who is one with the God of love, came down to the earth, and fulfilled the law with love. Jesus lived the exemplary life of keeping all the laws of God.

Even if He completely kept the law, however, He did not condemn those who failed to observe the law saying, "You have broken the law, and are on the way to death." Instead, He taught the people the truth day and night so that even one more single soul could repent of his sins and reach salvation, and without ceasing He worked and healed and set free those who were shackled with diseases, infirmities and demon-possession.

Jesus' love was outstandingly featured when a woman, caught in the act of adultery, was taken away and brought to Jesus by the scribes and the Pharisees. In the 8th chapter of the Gospel of John, the scribes and the Pharisees brought the woman to Him and asked Him, saying, *"Now in the Law Moses commanded us to stone such women; what then do You say?"* (v. 5) Jesus then responded saying, *"He who is without sin among you, let him be the first to throw a stone at her"* (v. 7).

By asking that question of them, He intended to awaken them that not only the woman but also they themselves, who accused her of her adultery and tried to find grounds for accusing Jesus, were the same sinners before God and that no one can dare to condemn the other. When the people heard it, they were convicted by their consciences and they went out one by one, beginning with the oldest even to the last. And Jesus was left alone, and the woman standing in the midst.

Jesus saw no one but the woman, and said to her, "Woman, where are those accusers of yours? Did no one condemn you?" She said, "No one, Lord." And Jesus said to her, "I don't condemn you, either. Go. From now on sin no more."

When the woman was brought and her unforgivable sin was revealed, she was oppressed with great fear. So, when Jesus forgave her, can you imagine the many tears she shed in deep emotion and thankfulness! Whenever she remembered this forgiveness and love of Jesus, she would not dare to break the law again nor could she sin anymore. This was made possible because she met Jesus who fulfilled the law with love.

Jesus fulfilled the law with love not only for this woman but also for all men. He did not spare His life at all and laid down His life for us sinners on the cross with the heart of parents who do not spare their lives to save their drowning children.

Jesus was blameless and unblemished and the only begotten Son of God, but He bore all the indescribable pains, poured down all His blood and water and laid down His life on the cross for us sinners. His crucifixion was the most touching moment of accomplishing the greatest love throughout the history of mankind.

When this power of His love comes upon us, we receive the strength to fully keep the law and are able to fulfill the law with love just the way Jesus did.

If Jesus had not fulfilled the law with love but instead judged and condemned anyone only with the law and turned His eyes from sinners, how many people could be saved in the world? As written in the Bible, *"There is none righteous, not even one"* (Romans 3:10), no one can be saved.

Therefore, God's children who have been forgiven of their sins by great love of God should not only love Him by keeping His commands with humbler heart but also love their neighbors as themselves and serve and forgive them.

Those Who Judge and Condemn Others by the Law

Jesus fulfilled the law with love and became the Savior for all mankind, but what did the Pharisees, the scribes and the teachers of the law do? They insisted on observing the law in actions rather than sanctifying their hearts as God wanted, but they thought they had completely observed the law. In addition, they did not forgive those who did not observe the law but judged and condemned them.

But our God never wants us to judge and condemn the other without mercy and love. Neither does He want us to take pains in observing the law without experiencing the love of God. If we observe the law but fail to understand the heart of God and fail to do it with love, it profits us nothing.

If I have the gift of prophecy, and know all mysteries and all knowledge; and if I have all faith, so as to remove mountains, but do not have love, I am nothing. And if I give all my possessions to feed the poor, and if I surrender my body to be burned, but do not have love, it profits me nothing (1 Corinthians 13:2-3).

God is love, and He rejoices in and blesses us when we do in love. In Jesus' time the Pharisees failed to possess love in their hearts when they observed the law in actions, and this profited them nothing. They judged and condemned others with the knowledge of the law, and it caused them to stay far away from God and resulted in crucifying the Son of God.

When You Understand True Will of God Embedded in the Law

Even in Old Testament times, there were great fathers of faith who understood the true will of God in the law. The fathers of faith including Abraham, Joseph, Moses, David, and Elijah did not only keep the law, but they also tried their best to become true children of God by diligently circumcising their hearts.

However, when Jesus was sent as the Messiah by God to let the Jews know about the God of Abraham, the God of Isaac, and the God of Jacob, they were not able to recognize Him. It was because they were blinded with the frameworks of the tradition of the elders and actions of observing the law.

In order to testify that He is the Son of God, Jesus performed amazing wonders and miraculous signs that were possible only with the power of God. But they could not either recognize Jesus or receive Him as the Messiah.

But it was different to those of the Jews who had good hearts. When they listened to Jesus' messages, they believed in Him and when they saw miraculous signs Jesus performed, they believed that God was with Him. In the 3rd chapter of the Gospel of John, a Pharisee named "Nicodemus" came to Jesus one night and said to Him as the following.

Rabbi, we know that You have come from God as a teacher; for no one can do these signs that You do unless God is with him (John 3:2).

The God of Love Waits for Israel's Return

Why then did most of the Jews fail to recognize Jesus who came to the earth as the Savior? They had formed frameworks of the law in their own thoughts believing that they loved and served God, and were not willing to accept the things that were different from their frameworks.

Until he met the Lord Jesus, Paul had firmly believed that

to fully observe the law and the tradition of the elders was to love and serve God. That's why he did not accept Jesus as the Savior but instead persecuted Him and His believers. After he met the resurrected Lord Jesus on the way to Damascus, his framework was completely broken into pieces and became an apostle of his Lord, Jesus Christ. From that time on, he would even give his life for the Lord.

This desire to keep the law is the innermost being of the Jews and the strong point of God's elect Israel. Thus, as soon as they come to realize God's true will embedded in the law, they will be able to love God more than any other people or race and be faithful to God with all their lives.

When God led the people of Israel out of Egypt, He gave them all the laws and the commands through Moses, and told them what He really wanted them to do. He promised them that if they love God, circumcise their hearts and live in accordance with His will, He would be with them and give them amazing blessings.

And you return to the LORD your God and obey Him with all your heart and soul according to all that I command you today, you and your sons, then the LORD your God will restore you from captivity, and have compassion on you, and will gather you again from all the peoples where the LORD your God has scattered you. If your outcasts are at the ends of the earth, from there the LORD your God will gather you, and from there He will bring you back. The LORD your God will bring you into the land which your fathers possessed, and you shall possess it; and He will prosper you and multiply you more than your fathers. Moreover the LORD your God will circumcise your heart and the heart of your descendants, to love the LORD your God with all your heart and with all your soul, so that you may live. The LORD your God will inflict all these curses on your enemies and on those who hate you, who persecuted you. And you shall again obey the LORD, and observe all His commandments which I command you today (Deuteronomy 30:2-8).

As God promised His chosen people Israel in these verses, He gathered His people who had scattered all over the world and let them take back their country in a couple of thousands of years, and set them high above all the nations of the earth. Nonetheless, Israel has failed to realize God's great love through the crucifixion and His amazing providence of creating and cultivating mankind but still follows the actions of observing the law and the tradition of the elders.

The God of love eagerly wishes and waits for them to abandon their own crooked faiths and to change and become true children as soon as possible. First of all, they have to open their hearts and accept Jesus who was sent by God as the

Savior of all mankind and receive the forgiveness of their sins. Next, they have to realize the true will of God given through the law and to possess true faith by diligently keeping the word of God through the circumcising of their hearts so that they can reach complete salvation.

I earnestly pray that Israel will restore the lost image of God through the faith that is pleasing to God and become His true children so that they can enjoy all the blessings that God has promised and dwell in the glory of the eternal heaven.

The Dome of the Rock, an Islamic Mosque
located in the lost holy city of Jerusalem

Chapter 4

WATCH AND LISTEN!

Toward the End Time of the World

The Bible clearly explains to us about both the beginning of the history of mankind and its end. For several thousand years now, God has told us through the Bible about His history of human cultivation. The history started with the first man on the earth, Adam, and will come to an end with the Lord's Second Advent in the air.

On God's clock of the history of cultivation of mankind, what time is it now and how many days and hours remain until the clock chimes the final moments of human cultivation? Now let's delve into how the God of love has planned for and set His will to lead Israel to the path of salvation.

Fulfillment of the Prophecies of the Bible in the Course of Human History

There are many prophecies in the Bible, and all of them are the words of the Almighty God the Creator. As said in Isaiah 55:11, *"So will My word be which goes forth from My mouth; It will not return to Me empty, Without accomplishing what I desire, And without succeeding in the matter for which I sent it,"* God's words have been fulfilled precisely so far, and every word will be fulfilled.

The history of Israel obviously confirms that the prophecies of the Bible have been fulfilled exactly without the slightest error. The history of Israel has been achieved just according to the prophecies recorded in the Bible: Israel's 400 years of bondage in Egypt and the Exodus; their entering the land of Canaan flowing with milk and honey; their kingdom's division into two – Israel and Judah and their destruction; the Babylonian Captivity; Israel's return to home; the birth of the Messiah, the Messiah's crucifixion; Israel's destruction and scattering to all the nations and Israel's re-establishment as a nation and independence.

The history of mankind is under the control of God the Almighty, and whenever He accomplished something important, He foretold men of God what would happen (Amos 3:7). God foretold Noah, a man who was a righteous and blameless in his time, that the Great Flood would destroy the whole earth. He told Abraham that the cities of Sodom and Gomorrah would be destroyed and he let the Prophet Daniel and the Apostle John know what would happen at the end time of the world.

Most of these prophecies recorded in the Bible have been exactly fulfilled, and the prophecies yet to be fulfilled are the Lord's Second Advent and a few things that will precede it.

Signs of the End of the Ages

Today no matter how seriously we explain that now is the end time, many people do not want to believe it. Instead of accepting it, they think those who are talking about the end of time are odd and try to avoid from listening to them. They think the sun will rise and set, people will be born and die and civilization will continue as it always has in the past.

The Bible records this concerning the end times, *"Know this first of all, that in the last days mockers will come with their mocking, following after their own lusts, and saying, 'Where is the promise of His coming? For ever since the fathers fell asleep, all continues just as it was from the beginning of creation'"* (2 Peter 3:3-4).

Whenever a man is born, there is a time for him to die as well. In the same way, just as it had a beginning, human history also has an end. When the time that is set by God comes, all things in this world will come to an end.

Now at that time Michael, the great prince who stands guard over the sons of your people, will arise. And there will be a time of distress such as never occurred since there was a nation until that time; and at that time your people, everyone who is found written in the book, will be rescued. Many of those who sleep in the dust of the ground will awake, these to everlasting life, but the others to disgrace and everlasting contempt. Those who have insight will shine brightly like the brightness of the expanse of heaven, and those who lead the many to righteousness, like the stars forever and ever. But as for you, Daniel, conceal these words and seal up the book until the end of time; many will go back and forth, and knowledge will increase (Daniel 12:1-4).

Through Prophet Daniel, God prophesied what would happen at the end of the ages. Some people say that the prophecies given through Daniel have been already fulfilled in the past history. But this prophecy will be fully accomplished at the last moment of the history of mankind, and is completely consistent with the signs of the last days of the world written in the New Testament.

This prophecy of Daniel is related to the Second Coming of the Lord. Verse 1 saying, *"And there will be a time of distress such as never occurred since there was a nation until that time; and at that time your people, everyone who is found written in the book, will be rescued,"* explains to us about the 7-year Great Tribulation that will take place at the end time of the world and about the gleaning salvation.

The second half of Verse 4, saying, *"Many will go back and forth, and knowledge will increase,"* explains the daily lives that are lived by people today. Conclusively, these prophecies of Daniel do not refer to Israel's destruction that took place in the year of 70 A.D. but to the signs of the end of time.

Jesus spoke to His disciples about the signs of the end of the ages in detail. In Matthew 24, He said, *"You will be hearing of wars and rumors of wars. Nation will rise against nation, and kingdom against kingdom and in various places there will be famines and earthquakes. Many false prophets will arise and will mislead many. Because lawlessness is increased, most people's love will grow cold."*

Today what is the world situation like? We hear news of wars and rumors of wars and terrorism is increasing day by day. Nations fight against one another and kingdoms rise against each other. There are many famines and earthquakes. There are numerous other kinds of natural disasters, and disasters caused by unusual weather conditions. Furthermore, lawlessness is increasingly prevalent all around the globe, sins and evils are rampant all over the world, and people's love is becoming cold.

The same is written in the Second Epistle of Timothy.

But realize this, that in the last days difficult times will come. For men will be lovers of self, lovers of money, boastful, arrogant, revilers, disobedient to parents, ungrateful, unholy, unloving, irreconcilable, malicious gossips, without self-control, brutal, haters of good, treacherous, reckless, conceited, lovers of pleasure rather than lovers of God, holding to a form of godliness, although they have denied its power; Avoid such men as these (2 Timothy 3:1-5).

Today people do not like good things, but love money and pleasure. They seek their own benefits and commit horrible sins and evils including murder and arson without hesitation or conscience. These things are taking place too much and so many things like this are going on around us that people's hearts have become ever increasingly numb to the point that nothing surprises the majority of people any more. Seeing all these things, we cannot deny that the course of human history is really going towards the end of time.

Even the history of Israel hints to us of the signs of the Second Coming of the Lord and the end time of the world.

Matthew 24:32-33 say, *"Now learn the parable from the fig tree: when its branch has already become tender and puts forth its leaves, you know that summer is near; So, you too, when you see all these things, recognize that He is near, right at the door."*

The "fig tree" here refers to Israel. A tree looks dead in winter but when spring comes, it sprouts out again and its branches grow and put forth green leaves. Similarly, since the destruction of Israel that took place in 70 A.D., Israel has seemed to completely disappear for some two thousand years but when the time of God's choosing came, it declared its independence and the State of Israel was proclaimed in May 14, 1948.

What is more important is that the independence of Israel indicates that the Second Coming of Jesus Christ is very near. Therefore, Israel should realize that the Messiah, for whom they are still waiting, came to the earth and became the Savior of all mankind 2,000 years ago, and remember that the Savior Jesus will come to the earth as the Judge sooner or later.

What then will happen to us who live in the last days according to the prophecies of the Bible?

The Advent of the Lord in the Air and the Rapture

About 2,000 years ago Jesus was crucified and resurrected on the third day breaking the power of death, and afterwards He was taken up into heaven and many people present witnessed His rising.

> *"Men of Galilee, why do you stand looking into the sky? This Jesus, who has been taken up from you into heaven, will come in just the same way as you have watched Him go into heaven" (Acts 1:11).*

The Lord Jesus opened the gate to salvation for mankind

through His crucifixion and resurrection, and then was lifted up into heaven and sat at the right of the throne of God and is preparing heavenly dwelling places for those who have been saved. And when the history of mankind ends, He will come again to take us back. His Second Advent is well described in 1 Thessalonians 4:16-17.

For the Lord Himself will descend from heaven with a shout, with the voice of the archangel and with the trumpet of God, and the dead in Christ will rise first. Then we who are alive and remain will be caught up together with them in the clouds to meet the Lord in the air, and so we shall always be with the Lord.

What a majestic scene it is when the Lord comes down into the air in clouds of glory accompanied by countless angels and heavenly hosts! Those who have been saved will put on the imperishable spiritual bodies and meet the Lord in the air, and then celebrate the 7-year Wedding Banquet along with the Lord our everlasting Bridegroom.

Those who have been saved will be lifted up into the air and meet the Lord, which is called the "Rapture." The kingdom of air refers to a part of the second heaven that God prepared for the 7-year Wedding Banquet.

God divided the spiritual realm into a few spaces, and one of them is the second heaven. The second heaven is divided again into two areas – Eden that is the world of light and the world of darkness. In a part of the world of light is a special space prepared for the seven years of Wedding Banquet.

The people who have adorned themselves with faith to reach salvation in this world full of sins and evils, will be taken up into the air as the brides of the Lord, and then meet the Lord and enjoy the Wedding Feast there for 7 years.

Let us rejoice and be glad and give the glory to Him, for the marriage of the Lamb has come and His bride has made herself ready. It was given to her to clothe herself in fine linen, bright and clean; for the fine linen is the righteous acts of the saints. Then he said to me, 'Write, "Blessed are those who are invited to the marriage supper of the Lamb."' And he said to me, 'These are true words of God' (Revelation 19:7-9).

Those who will be taken up into the air will be comforted for their overcoming the world with faith during the Wedding Banquet with the Lord, while those who will not be lifted up will suffer inexpressible suffering in tribulation by evil spirits that are driven out to the earth at the Second Coming of the Lord in the air.

The Seven Years of the Great Tribulation

While those who have been saved enjoy the 7 year Wedding Banquet in the air and dream of the happy and eternal heaven, the severest tribulation that is unparalleled in the history of mankind will cover the whole earth and horrible things will take place.

How then will the 7-year Great Tribulation start? Since our Lord comes back into the air and so many people will be taken up there all at once, those who will remain on the earth will be so panic stricken and shocked at the sudden disappearance of their family, friends and neighbors and they will wander about searching for them.

Soon they will realize that the Rapture that Christians talked about actually happened. They will feel horrified at the thought of the 7-year Great Tribulation that will come upon them. They will be overwhelmed with tremendous anxiety and sense of panic. And when drivers of the planes, ships, trains, cars and other vehicles are lifted up into heaven, a great multitude of traffic accidents and fires will occur, and buildings will collapse, and then the world will be filled with chaos and great disorder.

At this time a person will appear and bring peace and order to the world. He is the ruler of European Union. He will put the forces of politics, economics, and military organization together, and with the united power, he will keep the world in order and bring peace and stabilization to the societies. That's why so many people will rejoice at his appearance on the world stage. Many will enthusiastically welcome him, loyally support and actively help him.

He will be the antichrist referred to in the Bible who will lead the 7-year Great Tribulation, but for some time he will appear as a "messenger of peace." In reality the antichrist will bring peace and order to the people in the early stages of the 7-year Great Tribulation. The tool that he will employ to gain world peace is the mark of the beast, the '666' recorded in the Bible.

And he causes all, the small and the great, and the rich and the poor, and the free men and the slaves, to be given a mark on their right hand or on their forehead, and he provides that no one will be able to buy or to sell, except the one who has the mark, either the name of the beast or the number of his name. Here is wisdom. Let him who has understanding calculate the number of the beast, for the number is that of a man; and his number is six hundred and sixty-six (Revelation 13:16-18).

What Is the Mark of the Beast?

The beast refers to a computer. The European Union (EU) will set up their organizations by taking advantage of computers. By computers of EU each person will be given a barcode on the right hand or on the forehead. The barcode is the mark of the beast. All kinds of personal information each individual has will be put into a barcode, and the barcode be planted on his/her body. With this barcode planted on the body, the computer of EU will be able to monitor, watch, inspect, and control each one in detail wherever he is and whatever he does.

Our contemporary credit cards and ID cards will be replaced by the mark of the beast, "666." Then, people will not need cash or checks anymore. They will no longer have to worry about losing their possessions or being robbed of their money. This strong point will urge the mark of the beast "666" to spread to the whole world in a short time, and without this mark, no one will be able to be identified, but neither will he be able to sell or buy anything.

From the beginning of the 7-year Great Tribulation people will receive the mark of the beast, but they will not be forced to receive it. They will just be recommended to do it until the organization of EU is firmly established. As soon as the first half of the 7-year Great Tribulation is finished and the organization has become stable, then EU will force everyone to be given the mark and will not forgive those who will refuse to accept it. Thus, EU will bind the people through the mark of the beast and lead them as it wants.

In the end most of the people who will remain during the

7-year Great Tribulation will be confined to the control of the antichrist and the government of the beast. Because this antichrist will be controlled by the enemy devil, the EU will cause men to oppose God and lead them onto the path of evils, unrighteousness, sins and destruction.

By the way, some people will not surrender to the ruling of the antichrist. They are those who have believed in Jesus Christ but failed to be lifted up into heaven at the Second Advent of the Lord because they did not have true faith.

Some of them once accepted the Lord and lived in the grace of God, but later lost the grace and returned to the world, and some others professed their faith in Christ and attended church but lived in the worldly pleasures because they failed to possess spiritual faith. There are others who have just newly accepted the Lord Jesus Christ and some Jews are awakened from their spiritual slumber through the Rapture.

When they witness the reality of the Rapture, they will realize that all the words in both Old and New Testaments were true, and they will lament beating the ground. They will be captured by great fear, repent for not living by the will of God, and try to find a way to receive salvation.

Then another angel, a third one, followed them, saying with a loud voice, 'If anyone worships the beast and his image, and receives a mark on his forehead or on his hand, he also will drink of the wine of the wrath of God, which is mixed in full strength in the cup of His anger; and he will be tormented with fire and brimstone in the presence of the holy angels and in the presence of the Lamb. And the smoke of their torment goes up forever and ever; they have no rest day and night, those who worship the beast and his image, and whoever receives the mark of his name.' Here is the perseverance of the saints who keep the commandments of God and their faith in Jesus (Revelation 14:9-12).

If anyone receives the mark of the beast, he is forced to become obedient to the antichrist who opposes God. That's why the Bible emphasizes that whoever is given the mark of the beast cannot reach salvation. During the Great Tribulation those who know this fact will endeavor not to receive the mark of the beast to show the evidence that they have faith.

The identity of the antichrist will be clearly revealed. He will categorize as impure elements of the society those who will oppose his policy and refuse to receive the mark and purge them from the society for the reason of breaking the social peace. And, he will force them to deny Jesus Christ and to receive the mark of the beast. If they resist, severe persecutions and their martyrdoms will follow.

Salvation by Martyrdom for Not Receiving the Mark of the Beast

The torments for those who resist receiving the mark of the beast during the 7-year Great Tribulation are unimaginably severe. The torments are too oppressing for them to endure, so there will be found just a few who overcome it and get the last opportunity for their salvation. Some of them will say, "I am not abandoning my faith in the Lord. I still believe in Him from my heart. Torments are so overwhelming to me that I deny the Lord just with my mouth. God will understand me and save me" and then receive the mark of the beast. But their salvation cannot be given at all.

A few years ago while I was praying, God showed me in a vision how some of those who remain during the Great Tribulation will resist receiving the mark of the beast and be tormented. It was a really horrible scene! The tormentors skinned out, broke all the joints of the body into pieces, cut off fingers, toes, arms and legs and poured down boiling oil on their bodies.

During Second World War, horrible slaughter and torments took place and they conducted medical experiments on living bodies. The torments could not be compared with those of the 7-year Great Tribulation. After the Rapture the antichrist that is one with the enemy devil will rule over the world and have no mercy and compassion for anyone at all.

The enemy devil and the forces of the antichrist will persuade the people to deny Jesus in any way to drive them into hell. They will torture believers, but not kill them immediately, with very skillful methods of torment with all kinds of cruel methods. All kinds of torturing methods and up-to-date torturing devices used for the tormenting will bring believers utmost panic and pains. But only the terrible torments will continue.

The tormented people wish to be put to death soon, but cannot choose death because the antichrist will not kill them easily and they know well that suicidal death can never lead to salvation.

In the vision God showed me that most of these people could not endure the pain of the torture and submitted to the anti-Christ. For a time some of them seemed to endure and overcome the torture with strong will, but when they saw their beloved children or parents being tormented in the same ways they abandoned resistance, surrendered to the antichrist and then receive the mark of the beast.

Among those tormented people, quiet a few who have upright and truthful hearts will overcome those horrible torments and shrewd temptations of the antichrist, and die deaths of martyrs. Thus, those who keep their faith through martyrdom during the Great Tribulation can participate in the parade of salvation.

The Way for Salvation from the Upcoming Tribulation

When the Second World War broke out, the Jews, who had lived peaceful lives in Germany, never suspected that such horrific carnage as the slaughter of 6 million people was awaiting them. Nobody knew or could foresee that the Germany that had supplied them with peace and relative stability could suddenly change into such an evil force in such a short period of time.

At that time, not knowing what was going to happen, the Jews were helpless and they could do nothing to avoid the great suffering. God wishes for His chosen people to be able to avoid the upcoming disaster in the near future. That's why God recorded the end of the world in detail in the Bible and has let men of God warn of Israel of the coming tribulation and awaken them.

The most important thing for Israel to know is that this disaster of the Tribulation cannot be avoided, and instead of escaping from it, Israel will be caught up in the center of the Great Tribulation. I wish for you to realize that this tribulation will occur very soon and it will come upon you like a thief if you are not prepared. You will have to wake up from spiritual slumber if you are to escape from the horrible disaster.

Right now is the time that Israel must wake up! They

have to repent that they did not recognize the Messiah, and to accept Jesus Christ as the Messiah for all mankind, and to possess true faith that God wants them to have so that they will be raptured joyfully when the Lord comes back in the air.

I urge you to bear in mind that the antichrist will appear before you like the messenger of peace just the way Germany did for a time before the Second World War. He will offer peace and comfort, but then very quickly and totally unexpectedly, the antichrist will become the great force, a force that is growing in power at this time, and he will bring suffering and disaster beyond the imagination.

Ten Toes

The Bible has many prophetic passages that will happen in the future. In particular, if we look the prophecies recorded in the books of the great prophets of the Old Testament they tell us in advance not only about the future of Israel but also about the future of the world. What do you think is the reason? God's chosen people Israel has been, is and will be in the center of the history of mankind.

Great Statue Recorded in the Prophecy of Daniel

The Book of Daniel prophesies not only about the future of Israel, but also about what will have become of the world in the last days in relation to the end of Israel. In the Book of Daniel 2:31-33, Daniel interpreted the dream of King Nebuchadnezzar by the inspiration of God, and the interpretation was prophesying what would happen in the end time of the world.

You, O king, were looking and behold, there was a single great statue; that statue, which was large and of extraordinary splendor, was standing in front of you, and its appearance was awesome. The head of that statue was made of fine gold, its breast and its arms of silver, its belly and its thighs of bronze, its legs of iron, its feet partly of iron and partly of clay (Daniel 2:31-33).

What then do these verses prophesy about the world situation in the final days?

"The single great statue" that King Nebuchadnezzar saw in his dream is none other than European Union. Today the world is controlled by the two forces – the United States of America and the European Union. Of course the influences of Russia and China cannot be ignored. But, the United States of America and European Union will still be the most influential powers in the world in the spheres of economics and military strength.

Currently, EU seems to be a little weak, but it will increasingly be expanded. Today no one doubts this. Until now the USA has been exclusively the dominant nation in the world, but little by little EU will become more dominant throughout the world than the USA.

Just few decades ago, no one could imagine that the countries of Europe might be able to be unified into one system of government. Of course, the countries of Europe have discussed a European Union for a long time, but no one could be assured that they could transcend the barriers of national identity, language, currency and many other barriers in order to form one unified body.

But, beginning in the late 1980s, the leaders of the European countries started to seriously discuss the matter simply because of the economic concerns. During the Cold War period the main power to maintain dominance in the world was military strength, but since the Cold War came to a close, the main power shifted from the military power to economic strength.

To prepare for this the countries of Europe have been trying to unite and as a result, they have become one in an economic union. Now, one thing that remains to be done is political unification, bringing the countries together as one governmental system, and the situation now is spurring that on.

"That statue, which was large and of extraordinary splendor, and [whose] appearance was awesome," which Daniel 2:31 speaks about, is prophesying about the growth and activity of the European Union. It tells us how strong and powerful the European Union will be.

EU Will Come to Possess Great Power

How will EU be able to possess great power? Daniel 2:32 onward gives us an answer explaining with what the statue's head, breast, arms, belly, thighs, legs, and feet are made.

First of all, Verse 32 says, "The head of that statue was made of fine gold." This prophesies that EU will improve economically and command economic power through the accumulation of wealth. As prophesied here, EU will benefit and make great gains through economic unity.

Next, the same verse says, "its breast and its arms [were made] of silver." It symbolizes that EU will be socially, culturally and politically appear united. When a single president is elected to represent EU, it will accomplish political unity outwardly, and become wholly united in social and cultural aspects. However in a setting of incomplete unity, each member will seek its own economic benefit.

Next, it says, "its belly and its thighs [were made] of bronze." This symbolizes that EU will accomplish military unity. Each country of EU wants to possess economic strength. This military unity will be fundamentally for the purpose of economic benefit, which is the ultimate goal. In order to join in seizing the power to control the world through economic strength, there will be no choice but to become unified with the social, cultural, political, and military sphere.

Lastly, it says, "its legs of iron." This refers to another firm foundation to strengthen and support EU through religious unity. In the early stage, EU will proclaim Catholicism as its state religion. Catholicism will gain strength and become a mechanism of support to reinforce and maintain EU.

Spiritual Meanings of Ten Toes

When EU succeeds in unifying many countries in their economic, political, social, cultural, military, and religious sphere of influence, it will flaunt its unity and its power at first, but little by little they will begin to experience signs of discord and dissolution.

In the early stage of EU, the countries of EU will become united because they give concession to each other for mutual economic benefits. But, as time passes there will be social, cultural, political and ideological differences and discord arising among them. Then various signs of division will appear. Finally, religious conflicts will come out into the open – conflicts between Catholicism and Protestantism.

Daniel 2:33 says, "...its feet partly of iron and partly of clay." It means that some of the ten toes are made of iron, and the others of clay. The ten toes do not refer to "10 countries of EU." These refer to "5 representative countries believing in Catholicism and 5 other representative countries believing in Protestantism."
Just as iron and clay cannot be mixed and combined, the

countries in which Catholicism is dominant and those in which Protestantism is dominant cannot be fully united, that is, those that are dominating and those that are dominated don't mix.

As the signs of discord in EU increase, they will feel it increasingly necessary to unite the countries in religion, and Catholicism gains more power in more places.

Thus, for the economic benefits the European Union will be formed in the last days, and then will rise with enormous power. Later EU will unify its religion as Catholicism and the unity of EU become even stronger, and finally EU will come forth as an idol.

Idols are objects to be worshipped and revered by people. In this sense, EU will lead the world flow with great power, and reign over the world like a powerful idol.

The Third World War and European Union

As said above, when our Lord comes again in the air at the end time of the world, countless believers will be lifted up into the air simultaneously, and tremendous chaos will occur on the earth. Meanwhile EU will take the power and dominate over the world in the name of keeping the peace and order of the whole world in a short time, but later EU will oppose the Lord and lead in the 7-year Great Tribulation.

Later, the members of EU separate because they respectively will seek their own benefits. This will happen in the midst of the 7-year Great Tribulation. The beginning of this 7-year Great Tribulation, as prophesied in the 12th Chapter of the Book of Daniel, will happen in accordance with the flow of the history of Israel and the history of the world.

Just after the 7-year Great Tribulation commences, EU will increasingly gain tremendous power and strength. They will elect a single president of the Union. It will happen just after those who have accepted Jesus Christ as the Savior and received the right to become the children of God are instantly transformed and lifted up into heaven at the Lord's Second Coming in the air.

Most of the Jews, those who do not receive Jesus as the Savior, will remain on the earth and suffer in the 7-year Great Tribulation. The misery and horror of the Great Tribulation will be tremendous beyond description. The earth will be full of the most heartbreaking things including wars, murders, executions, famines, diseases, and calamities more extreme than anything in the history of mankind.

The beginning of the 7-year Great Tribulation will be signaled in Israel by a war that will break out between Israel and the Middle East. Excessive tensions have long lasted between Israel and the rest of the Middle Eastern nations and border disputes have never ceased. In the future this dispute will become worse. A severe war will break out because world powers will interfere in the affairs of oil. They will quarrel with one another to get the higher title and advantage in international affairs.

The United States that has been a traditional ally of Israel for a very long time will support Israel. The European Union, China, and Russia, which are against the USA, will ally with the Middle East, and then the Third World War will break out between both the parties.

The Third World War will be totally different from the Second World War in its scale. At the World War II more than 50 million people were killed or died as a result of the war. Now the power of modern weapons including nuclear bombs, chemical and biological weapons, and many others cannot be compared with those of the Second World War, and the results of their use will be unimaginably appalling.

All kinds of weapons including nuclear bombs and various up-to-dated weapons that have since been invented will be used mercilessly, and indescribable destructions and slaughters will follow. The countries that will have waged the war will be completely destroyed and impoverished. That will not be the end of the war. Nuclear explosion will be followed by radioactivity, and radioactive pollution, serious climate change and calamities will cover the whole earth. As a result, the whole earth as well as those countries that wage the war will be in a hell on earth.

In the middle, they will stop the nuclear weapons attacks because if nuclear weapons are used more, it would threaten the existence of all mankind. But all other weapons and the great multitudes of the armies will accelerate the war. The USA, China, and Russia will not be able to recover.

Most countries of the world will almost collapse, but EU will escape from the most devastating harm. EU promises China and Russia their support, but during the war, EU will not actively participate in the fighting so that it will not suffer as great a loss as others.

When many world powers including the USA suffer a great amount of loss and lose the power in the whirlwind of the unprecedented warfare, EU will become the single most powerful national alliance and will rule over the world. At first EU will simply watch the war progression and when other countries are completely destroyed economically and militarily, then EU will come forth and begin solving the war. The other countries will have no choice but to follow the decision of EU because they have lost all power.

From this point on, the second half of the 7-year Great Tribulation will start, and for the coming three and a half years, the antichrist, who is the ruler of EU, will control the whole world and canonize himself. And the antichrist will torment and persecute those who will oppose him.

The True Nature of the Antichrist Revealed

In the early stages of World War III several countries will have suffered great losses from the war and EU will promise economic support to them through China and Russia. Israel will have been sacrificed as the central focus of the war and at this time EU will promise to build the holy temple of God that Israel has been so longed for. With this appeasement by EU, Israel will dream of the revival of the glory they enjoyed in the blessing of God so long ago. As a result they too will be allied with EU.

Because of his support for Israel, the President of EU will be considered to be the savior to the Jews. The protracted warfare in Middle East will seem to come to an end, and they will again restore the Holy Land and build the holy temple of God. They will believe that the Messiah and their King, for whom they have waited for so long, has finally come and completely restored Israel and glorified them.

But their expectation and joy will fall to the ground soon. When the holy temple of God is reconstructed in Jerusalem, something unexpected will happen. This has been prophesied through the Book of Daniel.

> *And he will make a firm covenant with the many for one week, but in the middle of the week he will put a stop to sacrifice and grain offering; and on the wing of abominations will come one who makes desolate, even until a complete destruction, one that is decreed, is poured out on the one who makes desolate (Daniel 9:27).*

Forces from him will arise, desecrate the sanctuary fortress, and do away with the regular sacrifice. And they will set up the abomination of desolation (Daniel 11:31).

From the time that the regular sacrifice is abolished and the abomination of desolation is set up, there will be 1, 290 days (Daniel 12:11).

These three verses all allude to a single incident they have in common. This is the very incident that will happen at the end of the ages, and Jesus also spoke about the end of the ages with this verse.

He said in Matthew 24:15-16, *"Therefore when you see the abomination of desolation which was spoken of through Daniel the prophet, standing in the holy place (let the reader understand), then those who are in Judea must flee to the mountains."*

At first the Jews will believe that EU has reconstructed the holy temple of God in the Holy Land that they have considered holy, but when the abomination stands in the holy place, they will be shocked and realize that their faith has since been wrong. They will notice that they have turned their eyes from Jesus Christ and that He is their Messiah and the Savior of mankind.

This is the very reason that Israel has to be awakened now.

Unless Israel is awakened now, they will not be able to realize the truth at the proper time. Israel will realize the truth too late, and thus it will be irrevocable.

So I eagerly wish for you, Israel, to be awakened so that you may not fall to the temptations of the antichrist and receive the mark of the beast. If you are deceived by the smooth and tempting words of the antichrist promising you peace and prosperity and receive the mark of the beast, the "666," you will be compelled to fall into the path to irrevocable and eternal death.

What is more pitiable is that only after the identity of the beast is revealed, as prophesied by Daniel, will many of the Jews realize the focus of their faith has been wrong. Through this book, I wish that you will accept the Messiah already sent by God and avoid from falling into the 7-year Great Tribulation.

Therefore, as I have told you above, you have to accept Jesus Christ and to possess a faith that is proper in the sight of God. It is the only way for you to be able to escape from the 7-year Great Tribulation.

What a pity that you fail to be lifted up into heaven and are left behind on the earth at the Second Coming of the Lord! But fortunately you will find a last chance for your salvation.

I eagerly plead with you to accept Jesus Christ immediately, to live in the fellowship with brothers and sisters in Christ.

But even now is not too late for you to learn through the Bible and this book how you will be able to keep your faith in the upcoming Great Tribulation and find the way that God has prepared for your last opportunity for salvation, and to be guided to the very path.

Unfailing Love of God

God has fulfilled His providence for human salvation through Jesus Christ, and regardless of race and nation, whoever accepts Jesus as his Savior and does the will of God, God has made him His child and allowed for him to enjoy eternal life.

But what has happened to Israel and its people? Many of them have not accepted Jesus Christ and stay far away from the path to salvation. What a great pity it is that they will fail to realize the way of salvation through Jesus Christ even until the Lord comes again into the air and the saved children of God will be taken up from the earth into the air!

What then will become of God's elect Israel? Will they be excluded from the parade of the saved children of God? The God of love has prepared His amazing plan for Israel at the last moment of the history of mankind.

God is not a man, that He should lie, nor a son of man, that He should repent; has He said, and will He not do it? Or has He spoken, and will He not make it good? (Numbers 23:12)

What is the last providence that God has planned for Israel in the end of the ages? God has prepared the way of "gleaning salvation" for His elect Israel so that they can enter into salvation by realizing that the Jesus they crucified is the very Messiah whom they have looked forward to so long and thoroughly repenting of their sins before God.

Gleaning Salvation

During the 7-year Great Tribulation, because they have witnessed many people lifted up into heaven and come to know the truth, some people who will be left behind on the earth will believe and accept in their hearts the fact that the heaven and hell really exist, God is alive, and Jesus Christ is our only Savior. Moreover, they will try not to receive the mark of the beast. After the Rapture, they will be transformed in themselves, read the word of God recorded in the Bible, come together and have the worship services and try to live by the word of God.

In the early stages of the Great Tribulation many people will be able to lead religious lives and even to evangelize others because there will not yet be any organized persecutions. They will not receive the mark of the beast because they have already known that they cannot receive salvation with the mark, and try their best to lead lives that are worthy to gain salvation even during the Great Tribulation. But it will be really difficult for them to keep their faith because the Holy Spirit has left the world.

Many of them will shed a lot of tears because they will have no one to lead the worship services and to help them increase their faith. They will have to keep their faith without the protection and strength of God. They will mourn because they will have to regret that they have not followed the teaching of the word of God although they were advised to accept Jesus Christ and to lead faithful believing lives. They will have to keep their faith under all kinds of trials and persecutions in this world in which they will have difficulty in finding the true word of God.

Some of them will hide themselves deep in the remote mountains not to receive the mark of the beast, the '666.' They will have to search for roots of plants and trees and kill animals for food because they cannot buy or sell anything to gain food without the mark of the beast. But during the second half of the Great Tribulation, for three and half a years, the army of the antichrist will strictly and attentively chase the believers. It will not matter in what remote mountain they will hide themselves, but they will be discovered and taken away by the army.

The government of the beast will pick up those who have not received the mark of the beast and force them to deny the Lord and to receive the mark through severe torments. Finally many of them will surrender and have no choice but to receive the mark because of utmost pain and horror in the infliction.

The army will hang them on the wall naked and pierce through their bodies with a gimlet. They will skin the whole body from head to toe. They will torture their children before their eyes. The tortures that the army will inflict on them are excessively cruel so that it will be really difficult for them to die martyred deaths.

That's why just a few who have overcome all the tortures with the strong willpower transcending the limitation of human strength and died martyred deaths can receive salvation and reach heaven. Thus, some people will be saved through keeping their faith without betraying the Lord and sacrificing their lives in martyrdom under the control of the antichrist during the Great Tribulation. This is called "Gleaning salvation."

God has deep secrets that He has prepared for the gleaning salvation of God's elect Israel. It is Two witnesses and the place, Petra.

The Appearance and the Ministry of Two Witnesses

Revelation 11:3 says, *"And I will grant authority to my two witnesses, and they will prophesy for twelve hundred and sixty days, clothed in sackcloth."* The Two Witnesses are the very people that God has destined in His plan since before the ages to save His elect, Israel. They will testify to the Jews in Israel that Jesus Christ is the one and only Messiah that had been prophesied in Old Testament.

God has spoken to me about the Two Witnesses. He explained about them that they are not that old, they walk in righteousness, and they have upright hearts. He let me know what kind of confessions one of the Two makes before God. His confession says that he has believed in Judaism, but he heard that many people believe in Jesus Christ as the Savior and speak about Him. So, he is praying to God to help him discern which is correct and true saying,

Oh, God!

What is this trouble in my heart?
I believe all the things true
that I have heard from my parents and spoken
since I was young,
but what are these troubles and questions in my heart?

Many people speak and talk about the Messiah.

But only if someone can just show me
with sound and clear evidence
whether it is right to believe them
or to believe only what I have heard since I was young,
I will be joyful and thankful.

But I cannot see anything,
and to follow what those people are talking about,

I have to regard all the things meaningless and foolish
that I have kept since I was young.
What is really right in Your sight?

Father God!
If You will,
show me a person
who can establish everything and understand everything.
Let him come before me and teach me
what is really precise and what the real truth is.

As I look up to the sky,
I have this trouble in my heart,
and if anybody can solve this problem,
please show him to me.

I cannot betray from my heart all the things I have believed,
and as I contemplate on all these things,
if there is anybody who can teach and show them to me,
only if he can show me that it is true,
it won't be that I betray all the things
I have learned and seen.

Therefore, Father God!
Please show it to me.

Give me understanding on all these things.

I am troubled about so many things.
I believe that all the things I have heard until now are true.

But as I contemplate on them again and again,
I have many questions, and my thirst is not quenched;
Why is it so?

Therefore, only if I can see all these things
and can be sure of them;
only if I can be sure that it is not a betrayal
against the way I have walked until now;
only if I can see what really is the truth;
only if I can come to know all the things
I have been thinking of,
then I will be able to gain peace in my heart."

Therefore, only if I can see
all these things
and can be sure of them;
only if I can be sure that it is not a betrayal against the way
I have walked until now;
only if I can see what really is the truth;
only if I can come to know all
 the things
I have been thinking of,
then I will be able to gain peace in my heart."

The Two Witnesses, who are Jews, are deeply searching for pure truth, and God will answer them and send them a man of God. Through the man of God they will realize the providence of God's human cultivation and accept Jesus Christ. They will stay on the earth during the 7-year Great Tribulation and do the ministry for the repentance and salvation of Israel. They will receive the special power of God and testify Jesus Christ to Israel.

They will come forth fully sanctified in the sight of God, and do their ministry for 42 months as written in Revelation 11:2. The reason that the Two Witnesses come from Israel is because the beginning and end of the gospel is Israel. The gospel was spread to the world by the Apostle Paul, and now if the gospel again reaches Israel, which is its starting point, then the works of the gospel will be completed.

Jesus said in Acts 1:8, *"but you will receive power when the Holy Spirit has come upon you; and you shall be My witnesses both in Jerusalem, and in all Judea and Samaria, and even to the remotest part of the earth."* The "remotest part of the earth" here refers to Israel which is final destination of the gospel.

The Two Witnesses will preach the message of the cross to the Jews and explain to them about the way of salvation with the fiery power of God. And they will perform amazing wonders and miraculous signs confirming the message. They will have the power to shut up the sky, so that rain will not fall during the days of their prophesying; and they have power over the waters to turn them into blood, and to strike the earth with every plague, as often as they desire.

Through this many Jews will return to the Lord, but at the same time some others will be cut to their consciences and try to kill the Two Witnesses. Not only those Jews, but also many wicked people of other countries under the control of the antichrist will severely hate the Two Witnesses and try to kill them.

Two Witnesses' Martyrdoms and Resurrection

The power that the Two Witnesses have is so great that no one will dare to harm them. Finally the authorities of the nation will partake in killing them. But the reason that the Two Witnesses will be put to death is not because of the authorities of the nation, but because it is the will of God for them to be martyred at the ordained time. The place where they will be martyred is none other than the place of Jesus' crucifixion, and it implies their resurrection.

When Jesus was crucified, the Roman soldiers guarded His tomb so that no one might take His body. But His body was not seen later because He was resurrected. The people who will put the Two Witnesses to death will remember this and be worried that someone might take their bodies. So, they will not allow their bodies to be buried in a tomb but lay their dead bodies on the street so that all the peoples of the world can look at their dead bodies. At this sight, those wicked people who have been cut to their consciences because of the gospel the Two Witnesses preached will greatly rejoice over their deaths.

The whole world will rejoice and celebrate, and the mass media will spread the news of their deaths to the world through the satellites for three and a half days. After three and a half days the resurrection of the Two Witnesses will take place. They will be made alive again, raised up and lifted up into heaven in the cloud of glory just as Elijah was taken up into heaven in whirlwinds. This amazing scene will be broadcast all over the world and countless people will watch it.

And in that hour there will be a great earthquake, and a tenth of the city will fall, and seven thousand people will be killed in the earthquake. Revelation 11:3-13 describe this in detail as follows.

And I will grant authority to my two witnesses, and they will prophesy for twelve hundred and sixty days, clothed in sackcloth. These are the two olive trees and the two lampstands that stand before the Lord of the earth. And if anyone wants to harm them, fire flows out of their mouth and devours their enemies; so if anyone wants to harm them, he must be killed in this way. These have the power to shut up the sky, so that rain will not fall during the days of their prophesying; and they have power over the waters to turn them into blood, and to strike the earth with every plague, as often as they desire. When they have finished their testimony, the beast that comes up out of the abyss will make war with them, and overcome them and kill them. And their dead bodies will lie in the street of the great city which mystically is called Sodom and Egypt, where also their Lord was crucified. Those from the peoples and tribes and tongues and nations will look at their dead bodies for three and a half days, and will not permit their dead bodies to be laid in a tomb. And those who dwell on the earth will rejoice over them and celebrate; and they will send gifts to one another, because these two prophets tormented those who dwell on the earth. But after the three and a half days, the breath of life from God came into them, and they stood on their feet; and great fear fell upon those who were watching them. And they heard a loud voice from heaven saying to them, "Come up here." Then they went up into heaven in the cloud, and their enemies watched them. And in that hour there was a great earthquake, and a tenth of the city fell; seven thousand people were killed in the earthquake, and the rest were terrified and gave glory to the God of heaven (Revelation 11:3-13).

No matter how stubborn they will be, if they have a slightest goodness in their hearts, they will realize that the great earthquake and the resurrection and ascension into heaven of the Two Witnesses are the works of God, and give glory to God. And they will be compelled to acknowledge the fact that Jesus was resurrected by the power of God about 2,000 years ago. Regardless of all these occurrences, some wicked people will not give glory to God.

I urge all of you to accept the love of God. Up to the last moment God wishes to save you and wishes for you to listen to the Two Witnesses. The Two Witnesses will testify with great power of God that they have come from God. They will awaken many people about God's love and will for them. And they will guide you to grasp the last opportunity for salvation.

I eagerly ask you not to stand beside the enemies who belong to the devil who will lead you on the path to destruction, but to listen to the Two Witnesses and reach salvation.

Petra, A Refuge for the Jews

The other secret that God has destined for His elect, Israel, is Petra, a refuge during the 7-year Great Tribulation. Isaiah 16:1-4 explain about this place called Petra.

Send the tribute lamb to the ruler of the land, from Sela by way of the wilderness to the mountain of the daughter of Zion. Then, like fleeing birds or scattered nestlings, the daughters of Moab will be at the fords of the Arnon. Give us advice, make a decision; cast your shadow like night at high noon; hide the outcasts, do not betray the fugitive. Let the outcasts of Moab stay with you; be a hiding place to them from the destroyer. For the extortioner has come to an end, destruction has ceased, oppressors have completely disappeared from the land (Isaiah 16:1-4).

The land of Moab indicates the land of Jordan in the eastern side of Israel. Petra is an archaeological site in southwestern Jordan, lying on the slope of Mount Hor in a basin among the mountains which form the eastern flank of Arabah (Wadi Araba), the large valley running from the Dead Sea to the Gulf of Aqaba. Petra is usually identified with Sela which also means a rock, with the Biblical references in 2 Kings 14: 7 and Isaiah 16: 1.

After the Lord comes again into the air, He will receive the saved people and enjoy the 7-year Wedding Banquet, and then He will come down to the earth along with them and rule over the world during the Millennium. For the 7 years, from the Lord's Second Coming into the air for the Rapture until His coming down to the earth, the Great Tribulation will cover the earth, and for the three and a half years during the second half of the Great Tribulation – for 1,260 days, the people of Israel will hide themselves at the place prepared according to the plan of God. The hiding place is Petra (Revelation 12:6-14).

Why then will the Jews need that hiding place?

After God chose the people of Israel, Israel has been attacked and persecuted by numerous Gentile races. The reason is that the devil that always opposes God has tried to hinder Israel from receiving blessing from God. The same will happen during the end time of the world.

When the Jews realize through 7-year Great Tribulation that their Messiah and Savior is Jesus, who came down to earth 2,000 years ago, and try to repent, the devil will persecute them to the end in order to prevent the Jews from keeping their faith.

God, who knows everything, has prepared the hiding place for His elect Israel, through which He demonstrate His love for them and will not spare His considerate love for them. According to this love and plan of God, Israel will enter into Petra to escape from destroyers.

Just the way Jesus said in Matthew 24:16, *"Then those who are in Judea must flee to the mountains,"* the Jews will be able to escape from the 7-year Great Tribulation at the hiding place in the mountains, and keep their faith and reach salvation there.

When the angel of death destroyed all the firstborns of

Egypt, the Hebrews contacted one another quickly in secret and escaped from the same plague by putting the blood of the lamb on the two doorposts and on the lintel of their houses.

In the same way, the Jews will contact one another so quickly about where to go and move to the hiding place before the government of the antichrist starts arresting them. They will have known about the Petra because many evangelists have continually testified to the hiding place, and even for those who have not believed, they will change their minds and seek the hiding place.

This hiding place will not be able to accommodate too many people. In fact, many people who have repented through the Two Witnesses will fail to hide at the Petra and keep their faiths during the Great Tribulation and then die deaths as martyrs.

The Love of God through Two Witnesses and Petra

Dear brothers and sisters, have you lost the chance of salvation through the Rapture? Then, do not hesitate to go to Petra, the last chance for your salvation given by the grace of God. Soon horrible disasters will come by the antichrist. You have to hide yourselves at the Petra before the door of the last grace is closed by dint of the antichrist's interruption.

Well, have you failed to get the chance of entering Petra? Then, the only way for you to reach salvation and enter heaven is not to deny the Lord and not to receive the mark of the beast

"666." You must overcome all kinds of appalling tortures and die martyred deaths. It is not easy at all, but you will have to do it to escape from everlasting torments in the lake of burning fire.

I eagerly wish for you not to turn from the way to salvation by remembering the unfailing love of God all the time and to boldly overcome everything. While you are struggling and fighting against all kinds of temptations and persecutions the antichrist will inflict on you, we brothers and sisters of faith will earnestly pray for your triumph.

But our true desire is for you to accept Jesus Christ before all these things happen, and to be lifted up into heaven along with us and enter the Wedding Banquet when our Lord comes again. We are incessantly praying with tears of love that God will remember the acts of faith of your great fathers and the covenants He made with them and give you the great grace of salvation once again.

In His great love God has prepared the Two Witnesses and the Petra so that you may accept Jesus Christ as the Messiah and Savior and reach salvation. Up to the last moment in the history of mankind I urge you to remember this unfailing love of God who will never give you up.

Prior to sending you the Two Witnesses in preparation of the upcoming Great Tribulation, the God of love has sent a man of God and let him tell you what will happen in the end time of the world and lead you to the path to salvation. God does not want a single one of you to remain in the midst of the 7-year Great Tribulation. Even if you were to stay on the earth after the Rapture, He wants you to grasp and hold the last tie to salvation. That is the great love of God.

It will not be long before the 7-year Great Tribulation begins. In that greatest unprecedented tribulation throughout the entire history of mankind, our God will fulfill His loving plan for you Israel. The history of human cultivation will be completed along with the completion of the history of Israel.

Suppose the Jews were to understand the true will of God and to accept Jesus as their Savior right away. Then, even if the history of Israel recorded in the Bible should be corrected and written again, God would willingly do so. It is because God's love for Israel is beyond the imagination.

But many Jews have gone, go and will go their own ways until they meet the critical moment. God the Almighty who knows everything that will happen in the future has destined the last chance for your salvation and guides you with His unfailing love.

Behold, I am going to send you Elijah the prophet before the coming of the great and terrible day of the LORD. He will restore the hearts of the fathers to their children and the hearts of the children to their fathers, so that I will not come and smite the land with a curse (Malachi 4:5-6).

I give all thanks and glory to God who guides to the path to salvation not only Israel, His elect, but also all the peoples of the nations with His endless love.

Heaven I & II

A detailed sketch of the gorgeous living environment the heavenly citizens enjoy and beautiful description of different levels of heavenly kingdoms.

The Message of the Cross

A powerful awakening message for all the people who are spiritually asleep In this book you will find the reason Jesus is the only Savior and the true love of God.

Hell

An earnest message to all mankind from God, who wishes not even one soul to fall into the depths of hell! You will discover the never-before-revealed account of the cruel reality of the Lower Grave and hell.

Tasting Eternal Life Before Death

A testimonial memoirs of Dr. Jaerock Lee, who was born gain and saved from the valley of death and has been leading an exemplary Christian life.

The Measure of Faith

What kind of a dwelling place, crown and reward are prepared for you in heaven? This book provides with wisdom and guidance for you to measure your faith and cultivate the best and most mature faith.